Second Innocence

Second Innocence
Rediscovering Joy and Wonder

A Guide to Renewal in Work, Relationships, and Daily Life

John Izzo, Ph.D.

BERRETT-KOEHLER PUBLISHERS, INC.
San Francisco

Berrett-Koehler Publishers, Inc.
235 Montgomery Street, Suite 650
San Francisco, CA 94104-2916
Tel: (415) 288-0260   Fax: (415) 362-2512   www.bkconnection.com

Ordering Information
Quantity sales. Special discounts are available on quantity purchases by corporations, associations, and others. For details, contact the "Special Sales Department" at the Berrett-Koehler address above.

Individual sales. Berrett-Koehler publications are available through most bookstores. They can also be ordered direct from Berrett-Koehler: Tel: (800) 929-2929; Fax: (802) 864-7626; www.bkconnection.com

Orders for college textbook/course adoption use. Please contact Berrett-Koehler: Tel: (800) 929-2929; Fax: (802) 864-7626.

Orders by U.S. trade bookstores and wholesalers. Please contact Publishers Group West, 1700 Fourth Street, Berkeley, CA 94710. Tel: (510) 528-1444; Fax (510) 528-3444.

Berrett-Koehler and the BK logo are registered trademarks of Berrett-Koehler Publishers, Inc.

Printed in the United States of America

Berrett-Koehler books are printed on long-lasting acid-free paper. When it is available, we choose paper that has been manufactured by environmentally responsible processes. These may include using trees grown in sustainable forests, incorporating recycled paper, minimizing chlorine in bleaching, or recycling the energy produced at the paper mill.

Library of Congress Cataloging-in-Publication Data
Izzo, John B. (John Baptist), 1957–
    Second innocence : rediscovering joy and wonder : a guide to renewal in work, relationships and daily life / by John Izzo.
        p.   cm.
    Includes bibliographical references.
    ISBN 1-57675-263-1
    1. Conduct of life.   2. Innocence (Psychology).   I. Title.
BJ1595.I99 2003
170'.44—dc22   2003061716

FIRST EDITION
09 08 07 06 05 04   10 9 8 7 6 5 4 3 2 1

Text design by Detta Penna

To Leslie,
my partner in all things
and my greatest mentor in matters of the heart

Contents

Preface

This is a book about continually rediscovering the wonder and joy of being human. It is about seeing the world with the perspective of goodness, about making a choice to age without becoming cynical or jaded. It is a book for those who are old and those who are young, for those who have lost the zest for life and those who want to maintain it. It is a reminder for all of us of truths we already know but too often forget. It is a guide for maintaining hope and fighting cynicism. In it I suggest that, in a time when it would be easy to become cynical, we need to claim our innocence more than ever. And this innocence cannot deny the hard truths about life but must somehow incorporate them and allow us to choose to claim hope nonetheless.

I began writing this book when I was eight years old and, considering that I am now forty-five, you could say that makes me a pretty darn slow writer. It was in the summer of my eighth year that I had my first important lesson on living a purposeful, happy life.

On a hot, steamy August afternoon I was playing baseball in the streets outside our home in Staten Island, New York, when my mother called me to come home. Knowing it was too early for dinner, I protested, but she repeated the request with greater urgency. Once I was inside the house, she told me that my thirty-six-year-old father had died of a heart attack that afternoon. For a moment, I stood in silence. Then I asked to finish my game. I had not seen my father in six years and feelings of deep loss would not occur for many years.

Yet the lessons of that summer day were not lost on me. Though just a boy, I realized then that life was short, that our time on Earth is limited. Each day was a gift and could be lived fully or squandered. I also realized that it was wise to be intentional about the choices we make in our lives, that many people, such as my father, had missed much of the joy life offers.

Over the last thirty or so years, first as a minister, then as a business consultant, and finally as a writer and retreat leader, I have met thousands of people trying to find purpose and meaning in their lives, trying to figure out how to maintain loving relationships in an age of instant gratification, struggling to keep their faith in a world where cruelty and hardship challenge a belief in goodness, trying to renew their love for work. In those encounters I have seen many people who have lost their innocence about life and about themselves. The symptoms of this "loss of innocence" take many forms: cynicism about self and others, burnout at work, disillusionment in relationships, a loss of faith in God, a diminishment of hope, sarcasm about politics and organizations, and a more subtle sense that the wonder of daily living is slipping away. I have also met many people whose lives demonstrate that some spirits never fade, that it is possible to keep that sense of purpose and wonder—at work, in love, or in faith—and I think we all desire to be one of those people.

Somewhere along my own path of life, I lost a piece of my own innocence, a quality of spirit that the eight-year-old child possessed: an unbounded faith in the universe, an ability to be present and enjoy life's simple pleasures, an unshakable conviction that my actions could contribute to a better world, a pair of eyes to appreciate the beauty all around me and, most of all, a deep contentment. It was not so much that I was discouraged but that I sensed there was a deeper experience of renewal available to each of us.

This book is about what I have observed and discovered in the years since that day my father died, and what I believe to be the path to a more purposeful, joyful life, one filled with wonder and hope.

When this book was almost finished, I became aware that much of what I wrote is not new or earth-shattering, and I am glad of that. I don't believe it is ignorance of truths that keeps most of us from the full experience of human life; it is those truths we know but do not practice.

And now, as I look at the final manuscript, the best test of whether it was worth all the effort is this: I wish my father could read my book, and I wish I could have read it twenty years ago.

Rather than give you a formula for achieving second innocence, I will share with you stories, a collection of experiences from my life and the lives of people I have met over the last thirty years that illustrate the ways that we continually rediscover innocence in our lives. It is a very subjective journey, and, like all matters of the heart, such subjectivity is the only path to joy and wonder.

It is organized around finding renewal in four key areas of our lives: Daily life, work, relationships, and faith. These divisions are somewhat artificial, because certain core principles seem to bring us back to innocence and wonder in each area of living. There may be times when you may wonder what the chapters have in common or why one chapter has followed the next? What they all have in common is to show us the many ways in which we make the choice to find joy and wonder, to claim the ideal of hope. Each chapter provides a window into the many contexts in which we make the choice between innocence and cynicism.

Allow the stories in each section to speak their wisdom to you in whatever part of your life they find resonance. Don't worry about what "section" you are in, the messages will naturally find the parts of your life that are in need of them.

In the thirty years since that young boy learned of his father's early death, I have learned a great deal. Yet this book was not written by one who has arrived but by one who, like you the reader, continues on a journey of discovery that leads to a life well lived. These lessons are offered in the fervent hope that together we can discover again and again the joy and wonder of being human.

John Izzo
Lions Bay, British Columbia
November 2003

Acknowledgments

No one accomplishes anything without the help of others. A book like this one takes root in a lifetime of experiences shared with thousands of people. Yet a few people were particularly important in this effort and to those I wish to express my deep gratitude.

I send my love and gratitude to my wife and business partner, Leslie, whose very being has been my greatest teacher on how to hold on to hope. No words could ever thank or acknowledge how much my work and my person have grown for knowing you. Thanks for being who you are and for the hundreds of ways you contributed to this book, from important editorial input to your never-ending push for it to become ever deeper.

Jerry Eberts, whose loving and artful help as editor preserved my voice and made it richer. Your talent and your persona are a gift to those who believe in the power of words.

Steve Piersanti, my publisher, who helped this book find a deeper focus and who believed in it when it was but the seed of an idea.

My children, who have taught me more about innocence than I have passed on to them.

Melanie Bainbridge, for help on research and finding the occasional needle in a haystack.

My many friends who helped me focus and refine the ideas expressed in this book. They are too many to name but you know who you are.

My dear friend Rex Weyler for his own courage to change the world. Your friendship, love, and feedback helped me birth the thesis of this book.

I thank David Leidel who coached some of my early writing on this project and kept encouraging me to "tell my story."

Laurie Beth Jones, Beverley Kaye, Jeremy Ball, Bryan Evans, David Irvine, and Jeff VanderWielen, for your encouragement of the work found in this book.

My mother, who told me I could do anything and be anything if I wanted to badly enough, and my grandfather whose memory inspires me still.

Thank you to the thousands of people whose lives have reminded me that hope and innocence, not cynicism, is the one true path. You have reminded me that, if our eyes are open, wonder is everywhere.

Second Innocence:
A Choice to See Goodness

"We turn not older with years,
but newer every day."
—*Emily Dickinson*

There are only two basic ways to approach life; this is my conclusion after nearly half a century of living and meeting thousands
of people. The first vantage point is that of innocence and the second is that of cynicism. At any given moment, and on any given day,
each of us makes this choice many times. The way of innocence ush-
ers us to joy and wonder, while the path of cynicism takes us away
from the experience of being fully human. The path of innocence
promotes renewal, while the path of cynicism slowly erodes our
spirits.

Ironically, most of us began life with innocence: a native
enthusiasm, a sense of wonder, a firm belief in ourselves and others,

and a willingness to engage deeply in our days without fear or guilt. Yet as we age, whether we are twenty-five or seventy-five, many of us lose that sense of wonder, the faith and hope that give life purpose and meaning. This loss of innocence may be very subtle, but nonetheless very real. Such a loss of innocence happens in part because life is not easy, because others disappoint us and we disappoint ourselves, and because continually finding meaning in the various realms of life requires work. This book is about what it takes to stay innocent and how we can mature without losing our ideals.

Years ago Public Broadcasting made a film about people who had lived to be a hundred. The documentary sought to answer the question: Why do some people make it to a hundred while most do not? They pored through all the research to see if they could find an answer. Was it yogurt? Was it beans? Was it genes? Their conclusion was fascinating: Good genes and a healthy lifestyle can predict living well into your eighties; after that, there seems to be a subtler predictor of that extra ten or twenty years. They called it perseverance, a willingness to move on in spite of disappointment and to re-engage with life.

As if in poetic resonance with their theme, the film makers were interviewing one of their centenarians in her home and the phone rang. As the elderly woman listened, it became obvious she was receiving some very bad news. When she got off the phone, the film crew learned that she had just heard about the death of her eighty-year-old daughter. Shocked and sympathetic, the crew suggested they should come back and finish the interview another time. The woman paused for a moment and said, "No, you've come a long way, give me a moment and we will go on." And on they went, finishing up the interview, as she demonstrated the very quality that best predicted a century of heartbeats. They called it perseverance; I call it second innocence, a choice to claim the wonder and joy of living in spite of the fact that life is not easy.

Why Innocence?

This book did not start out as a book about innocence. It began as a book about experiencing renewal, rediscovering a life filled with more joy and purpose. But as I became more and more aware of what I and others were seeking, the word innocence emerged as an important core concept in our search for a life worth living.

Innocence comes from a Latin word—*innocentia*—which means to be harmless or blameless. *Nocens* is the Latin word for wicked, so innocence literally means to be "without wickedness."

In one sense, innocence is first and foremost to see the world not as wicked, but as good. In this way our view of the world can be blameless; we can choose to see the world as a good place, an Eden not lost but available.

But the word has a second meaning. Innocence is also a lack of sophistication, naïveté, a lack of self-consciousness, as in the phrase "she innocently asked a question." There is a sense that a person who is innocent comes to the world without self-consciousness, open to the possibilities that life offers. Innocent people are not jaded by the difficulties and sufferings of life, nor are they self-conscious because of guilt or shame.

Innocence and Childhood

Many of us associate innocence with childhood. Most children appear to have a natural joy and optimism that adults envy and long for. What is that childlike innocence?

Remember back to when you were a child. You likely remember something like this: Childhood is a world of sudden friendships and short sorrows. Put a group of young children together and they are fast friends and instant buddies. Disappoint a child and within a few hours he or she is smiling and laughing again. Children are good at letting go of things, which is why children can fight one day and be best friends again the next—or even within the hour.

As a child, you likely imagined unlimited possibilities for yourself and believed anything was possible. When I was young I imagined I would be the president one day and even created an imaginary cabinet of "advisors." My dreams were unlimited and unbounded. In some of my seminars, I ask participants about the wide-open possibilities they imagined for themselves when they were children. The roomful of adults suddenly lights up as people call out things such as ballet dancer, opera singer, painter, baseball player, senator, artist, and adventurer. Then I ask them what messages they received from adults in their life that contributed to the "loss" of those imaginative dreams. As the energy shifts perceptibly, the responses are things such as be realistic, you can't spend your life dreaming, you have to make a living, I once had dreams like that too but one day you will have to settle, and on it goes. A litany of how our innocence is lost.

When we were children we were also fully engaged in each moment of our day. Whatever was in front of us, we gave it our full attention. Think of how little time you spent as a young child worrying about the future or ruminating over past mistakes and how much time most adults spend worrying about what "may" happen and feeling remorse about what "has" happened. Yet the poets and sages have forever told us that it is only when we live in the "nick of time" (Thoreau) that life can be experienced fully.

Children are also naturally creative and spontaneous, willing to try anything, undaunted by the risk of failure or embarrassment. Researchers have looked at creativity and how it changes from kindergarten to fourth grade. It is both astounding and saddening that within those few short years children's scores on objective tests for creativity and risk-taking plummet. We go from being willing to do anything anytime, to calculating the risk of failure and embarrassment almost instinctively.

As well, when we were very young, we had a natural faith in the world. Children rarely wonder if life has meaning, they simply act as if what they do matters greatly. Most children believe they can and will change the world in some way.

Why Do We Need Innocence?

Several years ago, as I thought about my own life, I realized that my innocence had faded in a number of significant ways. When my career began, my head was filled with dreams of how my work would make the world a better place. Now, some days I wondered if the work I did made any difference at all. Earlier in my life I dreamed of great romantic love that would endure a lifetime. Now, with numerous relationships come and gone, betrayals scattered through my past, I wondered if true love, deep abiding love, was anything more than a fairy tale woven by great storytellers. At one time I had believed the world was becoming a better place and that it was our generation that would make the turn. But today, with forests disappearing and towers falling down in flames, I wondered sometimes if the human race was getting any better. At every turn, cynicism seemed to have overtaken innocence.

As I thought about the thousands of people I had met in my career and life, I saw this loss of innocence everywhere. Some people in marriages had long ago given up the idea that this would be "bliss" and had fallen into the comfort of an easy arrangement. Some were gutting it out in their careers until vacation or retirement. Some had given up on politics and written off the entire political system, and for some people their childhood faith had been shaken and their spirituality had slipped away. People were attending seminar after seminar in search of one more "life-changing" experience, all the while getting more discouraged at a deeper level. And in much more subtle ways, in our daily lives, mine included, the wonder and sheer joy of life's moments had become more elusive. It wasn't that life was not good, but that it seemed to offer so much more than many others and myself were experiencing.

At an even more profound level, it seemed to me that the entire planet had begun to lose its innocence. Leaders were talking for the first time in fifty years as if using nuclear weapons was an option; gone was the innocent belief that using these weapons meant the end of the world as we knew it. The polar ice caps were melting, but we read the headlines about global warming as we would a headline about the closure of the corner market, with a tacit acceptance that the loss of innocence, even the innocence of the biosphere itself, was inevitable. Newspapers were filled with scandals about corporate leaders who had bent the rules for their own personal gain. So I wondered, for myself and for my planet, was innocence truly lost or was it possible to capture it again? Was it possible to reclaim our ideals and our innocence without becoming childish? Could we choose to see wonder in the world without becoming naïve? Was it possible to age and not become cynical?

Innocence and Experience

The common belief is that as we age innocence is replaced by experience. As we gain experience we put aside our innocence and begin to see the world as it really is. Because of this belief, we tease those who are just beginning the journey about their naïve optimism and assure them that we were once as idealistic as they are. Whether it is the newlywed husband, the new young recruit at our firm, the fiery young activist fighting for justice, or the young teacher fresh out of college, we tacitly assume that their innocence will be replaced one day by experience, and that innocence must be put aside much as a child must put dolls aside for adult responsibilities. What might happen to us if we began to think of innocence as a quality we bring to our lives, a perspective and way of looking at the world, which is not replaced by experience but which influences our experience. That is, when we choose innocence as a frame to experience the world, then the qualities of hope, idealism, openness, and faith nurture the experience of wonder and joy in our lives.

So long as we operate on the assumption that innocence is a stage on the way to experience, we fail to grasp the extent to which our loss of innocence shapes our experience of the world. For example, the innocent newlywed enters marriage with the belief that his marriage will fulfill all of his hopes and dreams. When the new union fails to live up to his perfect hopes, he replaces innocence with experience and soon spends his nights at the pub trading marriage jokes with his buddies. All the while he may be unaware of the ways in which it is the very surrendering of his innocence and idealism that has shaped his experience of marriage. The new teacher begins her career fresh out of college filled with innocent idealism about how she will shape the hearts and minds of young people. But soon the harder realities of teaching begin to rob her innocence and she finds herself, almost imperceptibly, slipping into a comfortable seat in the teacher's lounge trading anecdotes with her older colleagues about how hopeless teaching truly is. All the while she is unaware that her choice to give up her innocence is shaping her experience and taking her ever further from the hopes she nurtured for her work in the world. The young idealist joins a political party believing he will "change the world." Those with more experience mock his tilting at windmills and assure him that the system is bigger than he is. If he is not careful, he will allow his innocence to be replaced by experience and find himself alongside others who read the daily news with disgust but scoff at the possibilities of changing the system. And the question arises: Did experience take away the innocence of these travelers or did their loss of innocence change their experience? Is the real challenge of life dealing with how the world comes to us or how we come to the world?

It is not that experience should not shape our idealism. In fact, our initial innocence must be shaped by our experiences. The newly-wed husband must recognize that marriage is hard work but at the same time hold on to his sense of hope about marriage. The new teacher must face the harder truths about shaping young hearts but at the same time hold on to a resolute belief in the power of a teacher to influence students. And the young activist must face the way in which the system resists change while continuing to claim his belief that courage and heart can overcome cynicism. To hold on to our innocence is a lifelong process and it is our ability to foster the quality of innocence that continues to bring us to the edge of what is possible in our lives and in our communities. That we may choose innocence and idealism while incorporating the harder experiences of living is the core premise of this book.

Why Second Innocence?

Although the perspective of being a child helps illuminate the meaning of innocence, second innocence is not about returning to childhood naïveté or discovering our "inner child." Quite the contrary, it is my contention that we cannot reclaim our first innocence. As wonderful as that innocence was, it was an unconscious innocence, born and bred in part by our ignorance about the world and its harsher truths.

One of the challenges we face in exploring the concept of innocence is the contrasting ways we see childhood. On the one hand, certain elements of being innocent are "childlike," but we associate other elements of innocence with being "childish." Many of us would like to be considered "childlike" but few of us want to be accused of being "childish."

This distinction is critical in understanding why I say we want to become innocent, but that it must be a second innocence. For example, it is childish not to worry at all about future consequences of present behavior, but it is childlike to get lost in the present moment. It is childish to believe the world is completely good and that there is no suffering, but it is childlike to have a basic faith that life is about something in spite of suffering. It is childish to pretend that you can hurt people and simply say you are sorry, but it is childlike to choose to put your sorrows and hurts behind you and embrace forgiveness.

Why Our First Innocence Must Die

It is my contention that the first innocence must die and pass from us. Why? Because the world is not all good, dreams are not unbounded, death and mortality wait for all of us, and some things about the future are worth worrying about.

As children we do not choose to be innocent; it is simply our nature. We live protected lives, like royalty, as parents protect us from the world's harsher truths. As we mature, our innocence meets disappointment, embarrassment, scientific fact, betrayal, financial concerns and so on, and our natural innocence slowly slips away from us. Some people keep a piece of it, but there are more jaded, faded, overly sophisticated, weary adults than there are joyous, childlike ones. There are also many grown-up Peter Pans still living the irresponsible, self-centered life of the child who wreak havoc on those who know them.

In this sense, the first innocence is like the first stage of romantic love that M. Scott Peck talks about in his book *The Road Less Traveled*. Peck says that "romantic love" is a wonderful collapse of the ego boundaries, a time when we believe that the other person we have met is our absolute soul mate and that he or she is "exactly" like us. He says that romantic love is nature's way of tricking us into mating. But at some point, inevitably, the ego boundaries reappear, we wake up and realize that this person is wholly "other" and not "us." Only then, when romantic love dies, is real love possible. This recognition does not diminish romantic love, Peck says, but gives it its rightful place. It is the precursor, an important and necessary precursor, to true love, which must incorporate the true "otherness" of the person we love.

This distinction is analogous to that in innocence. The first innocence is wonderful, it is beautiful, it is an unabashed embracing of all that is good in the world, but it ultimately must face the truth. In this way we all take the journey of the Buddha, who finally left his palace and discovered that there was great suffering in the world. Sheltered in the palace, he could never truly achieve joy. Only now, out in the world, is true innocence possible. Only when we are aware of the truths about life can our jobs, our loves, and our days be infused with deep purpose and meaning. Second innocence is a choice to reclaim our trust and faith in the world, not by denying what we know, but in light of what we know.

What Is Second Innocence?

Second innocence is a choice to see the world with the same eyes of wonder and faith with which we first viewed the world. It is a conscious choice to see the world with the perspective of goodness. Second innocence is not a naïve denial of the hard truths about life—suffering, death, betrayal, greed, loss, boredom—it is a willingness to choose to claim hope and wonder in a way that incorporates these truths. It is, above all things, our ability to be childlike without the destructive elements of being childish. It is the experience of finding ways to renew our love for our jobs, to deepen our relationship with others, to claim a belief in the possibilities of our influence, and to continually discover ways to renew our souls. It is about consistently taking a fresh look at our work, our relationships, and how we live our days, so that we maintain hope and do not fall into cynicism.

As adults, we live always in this tension between innocence and cynicism. Recently, I experienced a great example of this tension. My friend Adam started a new relationship with a woman. When we sat down for dinner he began to tell me about all of her wonderful qualities, their shared values, the feeling of meeting one's "soul mate," and how much he was enjoying getting to know her. Just then, he paused for a moment and reflected: "But I just can't get fully into it. I guess I've been around long enough now to know how it's going to end. My ex-wife and I felt this same way at the beginning, too!" This loss of innocence and movement toward cynicism keeps us from engaging deeply in the possibilities life offers. Hence the joke going around California now that on the first date a woman asks herself: "Is this the kind of man I want visiting my children on weekends?"

This tension between engaging and holding back is at the very center of the journey to second innocence: Can we love fully after we have failed at love or someone dear to us has betrayed us? Can we see the world of work with the same enthusiasm once we have been fired or had our business go bankrupt? Can we claim a life of integrity after we have "bent" the rules? Can we continue to have faith in the "goodness" of life, once we have lost a loved one to death or seen the horrors of the evening news? Can we live with wonder after disappointing others, finding out our spouse is imperfect, being hurt, and on it goes? Even more, can we keep experiencing life with childlike wonder and joy even as we age and mature?

And make no mistake, we cannot simply go back to our childhood innocence. We cannot pretend that these harder truths do not exist. We cannot become naïve again, but we can make a choice, a conscious choice, not to choose cynicism and bitterness. Second innocence requires us to make choices because, unlike the first innocence, it is an act of the will. The first one is simply given to us; the second one must truly be chosen, embraced, and nurtured. The first innocence is born and bred of childish ignorance; the second is traveled to, a journey that often includes a passage through a barren place. Whether in marriage, career, faith, or vocation, the second innocence rarely comes without the loss of the first.

Metaphorically, a passage to the second innocence often involves a trip through a desert. All the great heroes of mythology knew of this journey. These deserts can occur in a myriad of ways. The desert can be sitting at our desk for weeks staring at the abyss of career burnout. It can be when a marriage falls, sometimes for years, into nothing more than an enduring truce. It can be when we leave faith behind, but still hum the hymns when we hear them or pray to God in times of desperation. Or in less encompassing ways we may simply feel that the "zest" of life has slowly slipped away from us. In the end, it is a choice to leave the desert, to choose to be innocent again.

The metaphor may be imperfect, but what I have learned in my twenty-five years of meeting thousands of people is that the happiest, most joyful and purposeful people I know have an innocence about them. Not a childish innocence, not a pie-in-the-sky optimism, but an innocence that knows the harsh things that are true of the world and chooses nonetheless to live with hope.

Is Second Innocence Just for Old-Timers?

When I first began to write this book I had to ask myself an important question: Is second innocence only relevant to those in mid-life and beyond? Must one have lost the first innocence to need a second one? My conclusion is that the innocence I write about in this book is a way of living, not a stage of living, and therefore relevant to us at each stage of the life cycle.

Several years ago I was asked by one of the largest health care organizations in the United States to do a career renewal program for physicians. I was told that many of the physicians, especially those in mid and late career, were "burned out" and in need of recapturing the "spark." The first day of the workshop the room was filled with thirty physicians, and about two-thirds were forty years of age or older. To my surprise, the rest were young physicians, some just a few years out of medical school. Could they be losing heart already?

As we went around the room, each person spoke about why he or she had signed up for the program. The mid-lifers talked about how it was not as much fun as it used to be, how the joy of practicing medicine had slowly slipped away, and the hard truths of how the practice of medicine had changed. The younger physicians did not speak of being burned out but said they were already learning how tough it could be to maintain your enthusiasm and that they did not want to become like some of their older colleagues. They did not want to leave the work of renewal to be done once they had lost their spirit. Rather, they wanted to be proactive. I had similar experiences years before working with couples on renewing their relationships—some were already losing the spark while others wanted to deal with the work of renewal before they were in trouble. So it is with second innocence:The stories in this book help us at whatever stage we are at to discover the paths to renewing the experience of living.

But Do We Have to Work to Be Innocent Again?

Is second innocence a "feeling"? Is it simply an attitude or something we must work toward through the integration of certain practices and disciplines in our lives? It seems to me that the answer is yes to both questions.

On the one hand, second innocence is a simple choice, a decision to see life again with fresh eyes. It is a choice to wake up, to be aware of the joy all around us, to believe that the universe is friendly, to affirm the beauty of all things, to see possibilities in your marriage, to know your work makes a difference, to choose again the possibilities of your vocation, to reclaim your ideals, and to be more in the moment. It is not a choice we make once, but a choice we make hundreds of times every week.

Second innocence is a turning point, a simple choice, but it also involves a good deal of hard work and discipline to integrate this way of being into your life. Each day we must find ways to choose innocence over cynicism. This book is an exploration of the turning points we must experience as well as some of the practices we must embark upon, to integrate innocence more deeply into our lives.

Second innocence is not something we experience once in some great moment of awakening. These stories illustrate that whether we are young or old, we always live in the daily tension between idealism and cynicism, joy and despair, faith and unbelief, wonder and boredom, and the choice to see goodness or evil in the world we inhabit. So second innocence is the experience of claiming hope and wonder again and again in the different realms and moments in which our lives are lived.

Innocence

I am innocence
Staring up at you with a bashful smile
Biting my lower lip
As a curl twists around my finger
Will you kiss me?
I am anxious and eager
You bend
For your mouth to meet mine
I jump up and run
Laughing joyously, hair flying
Bare Toes
Prancing across open fields
Clouds drift slowly overhead
Enveloped in the afternoon sky
Myriad sun sprinkles caress my skin
And you begin the chase
Catch me if you can

—Shelley Langstaff

PART I

Rediscovering
Wonder
in the
Daily Journey

A friend of mine used to say that the problem with life is that it is "so daily."

What he meant was that it is how we live and approach each day that ultimately determines the quality of our lives. In this same way, the choice to move toward innocence rather than cynicism is one that we make each day, and often many times during the same day.

We don't rediscover joy and wonder through one large choice we make but hundreds of smaller ones. It is something akin to a silly riddle my kids used to ask me: "How do you eat an elephant?" One bite at a time!

This first section explores the mindsets that are required to find joy and wonder in each day, to discover a second innocence. It begins with stories about figuring out what really matters to us and then explores some ways of thinking about life that seem to facilitate innocence: Dealing with detours, letting go, opening up to awe and wonder, living with courage, and making time for our favorite subjects.

The principles found in these chapters set the stage for a deeper exploration of how we rediscover joy and wonder in the context of work, relationships, and spirituality.

I

Most of Life
Is Rowing

My grandfather was a man who lived a rich life.
A shipbuilder by trade, he was one of eleven children born in rural Nova Scotia. Although our family had been in Nova Scotia since 1746, my grandparents moved to New York in search of work during the Great Depression.

Grandfather was a quiet man, a deeply religious man, and, perhaps most of all, a person of significant character. Of all the people in my family, alive or dead, he lives on in mythology. Whether in stories of kneeling by his bed to pray before sleep or inviting homeless people home for dinner during the Great Depression (even though he was barely working himself), he is remembered as a good worker, a good father, and a caring human being. From him I gathered the simple phrase "good tired" to describe the experience of a day well spent.

Once when I was in high school, my grandfather invited me to go on a rowing trip with him. He loved the sea and told me that this particular evening promised a glorious sunset. "Would you be interested in going on a rowing trip with me to visit a tiny cove I'm sure you've not seen?" he inquired. Looking outside, wiping the sweat from my teenaged forehead, I suggested that 95 degrees was not the perfect time for a long rowing trip and said another time would be better. "Ah," he said, "another time is for young men. Let's do it now."

With that clarity of perspective, off we went on what would turn out to be a nonstop row of more than an hour. Given that he was in his seventies and I a mere fifteen, the rowing naturally fell on my shoulders. All during our trip to that cove, he was chiding me to go faster else we miss the promised sunset. "Chop, chop," he piped up. Sweating profusely, I diligently rowed until more than an hour had passed and we turned a corner beyond a tiny point of land and into the promised cove. Moments later, the sky burst into an orange-purple blaze. My grandfather was right, the cove and the sunset were both breathtaking. The scene is one I will never forget.

We were there, however, for no more than a couple of minutes when my grandfather said, "Well, let's head back now."

Incredulous, I protested. "Granddad, you were right, it is beautiful here. But look at me, I'm dying—let's stay for a while."

"No," he said, "they'll have made dinner for us and we're already late. We ought to think of others, not just ourselves. Besides, we've seen it and this beautiful sunset will follow us home."

Hands on the oars, I began the journey back. With each pull I renewed my complaining: "It was nice, but not worth all that rowing. . . . This boat is too old and needs new oars. . . . The current's too strong today. . . . You're the big shipbuilder—why don't you take a turn rowing?" On and on I went. My grandfather merely sat quietly, enjoying the sunset.

Finally, after about thirty minutes he gazed at me and quietly said, "John, put the oars down, would you?"

With the oars in the boat he stared me in the face: "I want to tell you something today, something I very much hope you will remember. John, most of life is rowing and if you don't learn to be good at—and enjoy—the rowing, you will grow up to be a very unhappy man. Now put your hands on the wood and take me home."

I would love to tell you that the scales fell from my eyes in that moment and my life was lived differently from then until now. But that would not be true. At the time, those words seemed like the babblings of an old shipbuilder about to make his last sail. But thirty years have passed and I know now what he meant.

Life is mostly rowing. There are, of course, moments of ecstasy, but most of life is made up of simpler moments. A walk on the beach, a glancing view of a beautiful cornfield out an airplane window, the first time you see your child steal a base, a conversation where you know your words helped a friend, lying in a tent by a river with the few people you love most, the good feeling at the end of a hard day at work when you know your efforts were not in vain. It is precisely our ability to be present and enjoy those moments that makes life worth living. We can spend our entire lives trying to get from one big sunset to the next and miss a whole lot of great living in between. Sure those great sunsets are wonderful, but they are the icing, not the cake.

The big things do not determine our success in the many realms of our life. Marriages are not built on the big anniversary trip to Hawaii or the special gift that marks a date. It is in the rowing that marriages are made and broken, in the daily honoring of life together. Parents do not raise children well because of the camping trip taken once each year to provide "quality time." Rather it is in the rowing moments, simple exchanges that occur thousands of times over the years that our children learn the lessons they will need to live a life uncommon. Leaders do not earn their stripes at the annual meeting when they give a rousing speech that inspires the masses, but in the daily way their rowing inspires a sense of pride and respect among those whom they lead.

But how do we begin to get better at the rowing and to appreciate the simpler pleasures it has to offer? How do we reclaim the innocence, faith, and wonder with which we were graced when we came into the world?

It seems to me that it begins with realizing that life is not about where we are going as much as it is about being where we are. How much of our lives are lived with the future as our focus—saving for retirement, waiting for the weekend, counting the days until vacation, looking forward to graduation, the next promotion. We seem destined to believe life will be better when we finally get *there*.

When we choose to believe that each moment, however simple, offers as much to us as the great shining moment of ecstasy, we begin to experience our lives in a different way. It is not that those moments of supreme satisfaction are unimportant; it is that most of life is spent rowing to and from the tiny cove and the rowing offers us just as much as the destination.

What part of the rowing must you pay more attention to? Are you enjoying the moments of your life fully or waiting for some future sunset when life will be what you desire it to be?

Enjoy the Journey

For thirty years since that rowing trip, as a minister, father, writer, husband, workshop leader, friend, and corporate advisor, I have tried to understand the lessons of that sunset. This book is a set of anecdotes, experiences, and reflections on how to rediscover the joy and wonder of life, the attempt of one person to reclaim the innocent faith and sense of purpose that gives life richness.

At this moment I find myself thinking back on my life, trying to recall the moments that stand out. To my surprise they are not my college graduation with honors, the speeches given before thousands of people, the day I held my first published book. Instead, I think of the cove with my grandfather, an afternoon nap in a tent with the wind gently blowing and cooling my face as my entire family slept beside me, a ride with my friend Steve in an old red canoe decades after my grandfather's trip, the e-mail I got last week from a person saying that something I had written had touched him deeply, and that my father would be proud of me. The moments are almost all moments of "rowing," simple pleasures that have come together to create a rich and meaningful life, a life of awe and wonder.

I have come to a place in my life where I have begun to experience what I call second innocence, a renewed sense of faith, hope, idealism, happiness, wonder, joy, and destiny. It is my hope that in sharing my journey of rowing, and the stories of those I have met along the way, your imagination will be captured and your life experienced with a fresh set of eyes.

2

Full Speed Ahead in the Wrong Direction

𝒜 𝒻𝓇𝒾𝑒𝓃𝒹'𝓈 𝑔𝓇𝒶𝓃𝒹𝒻𝒶𝓉𝒽𝑒𝓇 𝓊𝓈𝑒𝒹 𝓉𝑜 𝓈𝒶𝓎: "I'm going at full speed, but I'm heading in the wrong direction." His words could be the inscription that describes many people's lives: lots of activity, plenty of busyness, full speed ahead—but not focused on what really matters. Indeed, what appears to be a loss of innocence and a descent into cynicism may actually be a failure to focus our lives on what really matters to us. If we are to continue to come to the world with a sense of innocence and hope, we must find a deep conviction about what is truly important to us.

What really matters to us seems like a simple enough question that ought to be easy to answer. But what really matters to us is often harder to realize than we might suppose, hidden as it may be beneath years of habit, should do's, inherited beliefs, societal values, and a plain old lack of paying attention. Trying to discover what really matters to us and unearthing what our truest priorities are often takes some very intentional digging. And surely to truly reclaim our ideals and live a life of wonder, we must get more deeply in touch with what really matters most to us.

Meister Eckhart, the Christian mystic and writer, once said: "As human beings we have so many skins and know so many things, but we do not know ourselves." Indeed, many tragedies of literature have been written about characters that somehow missed their true nature. You may recall Arthur Miller's play *Death of a Salesman* about the tragic Willie Loman, whose years as a salesman produced a man with a deep, ongoing sense of failure. The play ends with his suicide and a scene at the graveside where Willie's son Biff muses about how his father had always loved working with his hands, but instead lived the life of a salesman. "He had the wrong dreams," Biff muses. "The man didn't know who he was."

Most of us will not end up like Willie Loman, living a lifetime in opposition to our truest tendencies, but in subtle ways we echo that life. When we fail to become aware of what really matters to us, when we fail to notice the rhythms of our life, we can easily wind up feeling as if we are going at full speed in the wrong direction.

Wake-Up Calls

Sadly, many of us never really ask what matters most until we get a wake-up call. Wake-up calls can happen in a number of ways: a health scare, a relationship breakup, or a job loss. I have watched many friends go through wake-up calls. A friend who is a fellow writer got a wake-up call a few years ago. Returning from one of many business trips away from home, his wife announced that she had decided to start a chicken farm. Taken aback, my friend inquired further. "Yes," his wife added, "and I will begin with two roosters and a hen."

A bit confused, my friend said, "Honey, I don't know much about chicken farming, but doesn't it take just one rooster to service one hen?"

"Not if one of the roosters travels a lot," his wife answered. Needless to say, he was awake. The question of whether work mattered more than family begged for an answer.

Another friend was a senior editor at *INC Magazine*. About two years ago, David Young became very ill and it looked, for a time, as if he might die suddenly. Lying on a gurney in a dark hospital room, he did what thousands of human beings have done in similar circumstances: He began making a list. It was a list of all the things he wished he had spent more time doing, all his regrets, all the things he would surely do or change if he had more time. Lying there in the hospital, what really mattered to him became very clear. Suddenly, with almost Zen-like clarity, he knew what his priorities were and also that there were many things he had put a great deal of energy into that were not nearly as important as he thought they were.

My dear friend had a very fortunate turn of events. The doctors were proven wrong, he was not dying, and now he had a bigger problem; he was going to live, but he had the list!

For some time all he could do was carry it around with him in his pocket. As he studied the list he discovered that many of the things on the "I wish I had done" list had not been done because of fear. Most of them involved some perceived amount of "risk," however small.

For the last year the list has come to focus his life and his time in a new way. His actions have become more intentional because he has answered the question of what really matters to him.

Last time we talked, he told me about his newly adopted ten-year-old son (one of the things that was on the list) and a foundation he started in his father's name (while his father is still alive). This was also on his list: Give back to the world.

Hearing his experience, I began to wonder why we wait to make such lists until we are confronted by our mortality. Why does a man wait until his wife announces she is leaving to think deeply about the kind of husband he has become? What is it about us that allows us to forget that we are all terminal, that the moment of our death is always imminent? I think of all the moments in my own life when mortality seemed closer: when a younger friend died suddenly, when the airplane I was on was rocked with turbulence, when I had an ongoing abdominal pain and my trusted family doctor sent me for extensive tests, his face somber as I'd never seen it before.

Each time, at least in my head, I have begun to make my own list, and each time, once the heat was off, the list somehow took a backseat to whatever fires were calling for water at the time.

How do we become clear on what is truly important to us? How do we discover our deepest values and desires? How do we keep these in front of us and make sure they guide us in our daily choices?

One way is to make the lists before we have to. We could make lots of lists that would help clarify what really matters to us, but here are a few to get you started. Pretend this is your last day of living and all you have time to do is complete one final assignment, to answer the following questions in list form:

- What do you regret not doing because of fear?
- What do you wish you had put more time and energy into?
- What do you wish you had put a lot less time and energy into?
- What was always on your "someday" list that you now wish you had done?
- As you think about your daily experience of life, what qualities do you wish there were more of and what qualities do you wish there had been less of (more time for self, more community, more kindness, more play, more service)?
- What is your deepest regret in terms of the type of person you never became (e.g., a kind person, a generous person, a truthful person, a strong person, a courageous person)?
- Answer this: If I had more time I would love to learn to . . .

REDISCOVERING WONDER IN THE DAILY JOURNEY

Put some thought and effort into the lists and take your time, watch the pattern that emerges and begins to inform you as to what really matters to you. Carry the list around with you, as my friend David did, and see what happens.

What Matters: The Little Things

In a way there are two dimensions to what matters to us. One dimension has to do with the "big things" in our lives. What legacy do we want to leave? What regrets do we have in terms of the overall focus of our lives? These often take the form of desires, latent ideals such as "I wish I had been more focused on relationships," "I wish I had pursued a career that made a difference in the world as opposed to a mere focus on wealth," and so forth. These are important things to notice because our loss of innocence often comes about because we have lost touch with what truly matters to us. But there is another dimension to what matters to us that is much more in the "now."

As we go through our days there are activities that energize and activities that enervate us. Enjoying the journey has a great deal to do with noticing the daily rhythms of our life.

My grandfather was one of those people who enjoyed the journey even though he never accomplished any large feats of greatness. When he was older he would sometimes sit down in his easy chair and comment about how fatigued he was. Such a comment was usually followed with a smile and the words, "But it's a good tired." My grandfather seemed to recognize that some days offer that experience of a "good tired," while others leave a taste of pure exhaustion.

A way to become more alert to what matters to us in the little things is to notice those "good-tired" days when you have them. What made it a good-tired day? What things were present in that day that energized you and made the journey more enjoyable? It is also helpful to notice the "bad-tired" days and become aware of the things that drain us. Simply write them down, notice, and let that awareness begin to influence your choices.

Here is a simple example. One of the things I have noticed about myself is that on my "good-tired" days I usually have been outside or been physically active in some way. It is rare for me to have a true experience of good tired when that simple value is not respected. When I make lists of the "big" things that are important to me, getting outside and taking short walks never makes the list. But if I notice the daily rhythm of my life, it seems to be one of the simple things that help me enjoy the journey. Knowing what matters to us, in the big and the little things, is critical if we are to reclaim the wonder of life, and uncovering what matters to us begins with the courage to ask the right questions.

A mentor of mine used to say, "The answers we find at mid-life don't matter very much, but that we ask the questions is profoundly important." That is, each of us will answer that question in our own way: What really matters to us? But if we fail to answer these questions the consequences can be devastating to the soul.

In one of my spirit workshops, I met a woman in her early forties whose son had just gone away to college. Her son was a junior, named after his father, and so for years she had to live with two men with the same first name. To stop the confusion she started calling her husband Mr. Jackson. The habit became an institution and for almost 18 years she referred to him that way. She and her husband drove their only son to his dormitory three hours from home. It was a sad day for her, but she knew she had done her job, given it her best and the time had come to let go.

As she got in the car to drive home she looked over at her husband and innocently said what came to her mind: "Well, I guess I won't have to call you Mr. Jackson any more." A torrent of tears poured from her husband's eyes and he bent over from the release of a deep well of feelings he didn't even know he had. He sobbed the uncontrollable tears of deeply held grief. She told me that, on reflection, she realized her husband had not asked what mattered most to him and put off connecting in a deep way with his son; he had not been intentional. In the car that day, after her simple statement of the obvious, he knew it was too late. Full speed ahead, but in the wrong direction!

So here is a simple reflection, something to do in winter when the cold sends you inside, to think about in the car as you drive alone: What really matters to you? What are the big things that matter to you and what are the more "daily" things that seem to bring you a life of wonder and joy, that inspire the much-sought sensation of childlike innocence? What are the things you keep putting off, the urgent things that edge out the truly important things? What are some of the things that matter to you deeply but have lost a place of priority in your current life?

Write them down, carry them around with you as my friend David did, and make sure you look at them as often as you look at your daily to-do list. And when your life is going full throttle—calendar full, all-out, without a moment to spare—make sure you are focused on the things that really matter.

3

Reclaiming What
We Left Behind

This is not a book about recapturing one's childhood,
nor is second innocence about becoming a child wonder. We may
think of children as being innocent, but the experience of innocence
is a way of being, a chosen state of mind—and one that can be experienced at any stage of life.

One of the things our own childhood can teach is to help us
remember the things that naturally animate our souls. Anyone who
is a parent knows that each child, even when raised by the same parents, has his or her own style, a way of being in the world that is
unique. Sometimes we will even say things such as "It is hard to
believe that those two came from the same parents." Mothers often
sense the differing temperaments of their children in the very first
days, the way they breast-feed, the way they cry. Later, each child's
particular style begins to take form in the things that the child likes
to do, how the child interacts with others, the classes enjoyed in

school, the hobbies chosen and, perhaps most of all, in the things the child chooses to do when no one requires anything at all.

Remembering these natural inclinations is critical to capturing the spirit that we had in the beginning of our lives. If part of second innocence is the reclaiming of the things from which we turned away, then remembering what we loved to do as children is one way of connecting to our truest selves.

Over the past seven years, I have asked thousands of people in my workshops to tell me what they loved to do as children. The instructions are simple: fill the page with all the things you can remember loving to do when you were young. In many cases, the faces of people exploring this simple question light up as they recount the passions of childhood. Yet this recounting is often done with the cynicism of lost innocence, whereby we wistfully speak of climbing trees, playing with dolls and friends, chasing chipmunks, sleepovers—all with a combination of glee for having once been so free and a sigh of resignation that adult life is simply not that way. Many people notice how much alignment there is between the things they loved as children and the things they enjoy as adults. Still others discover hints, important and profound hints, about the parts of themselves that they have left behind, parts that must be dusted off if we are to reclaim our ideals and experience the joy of living.

Consider my friend Jeff VanderWielen. Jeff grew up in rural Wisconsin, far from the sophistication of urban life. He spent hours exploring the tree lines between farms, a place where rocks were often found. Many of those rocks had fossils and he spent hours looking up the fossils in an encyclopedia. He remembers being an explorer and a learner; he liked to go and find out about things, to explore them fully, to solve the puzzle.

Years had passed since those early Wisconsin roots and the child had given way to a middle-aged man. His work life began with a short stint as a welder, then a job with Youth for Christ, college, a doctoral program and eventually a senior job at a large management consulting firm. Jeff could feel his innocence fading, his work becoming drab and uninteresting. Then he remembered young Jeff, who spent hours exploring and learning at the tree lines. My friend began to remember who he truly was. He realized that his happiest moments in consulting were the times when he was most like that young boy sifting through rocks to find another fascinating fossil, the feeling of adventure, of going out on a mission to discover something. He chose to reclaim this and commit to a path that would allow him to be more of a learner, to respect his natural gift for research and not merely the practical need to "get things done and be secure." Specifically, he began to focus on assessment centers and measurement, the consulting equivalent of solving a puzzle. Jeff is never so happy as when we he is trying to solve a riddle.

Through the years of leading others through these questions, I have had many opportunities to remember my own childhood. Two important things have emerged. As a child I loved sports and was a huge baseball fan. My grandmother, who lived with us, had been a Brooklyn Dodgers fan, and her passion for baseball coupled with a neighborhood full of baby-boomer boys put me on a path to a love of sports. Yet the thing I remember most was my baseball card collection. For years I collected hundreds of baseball cards, trying to collect all the players on each of the teams. I prided myself on knowing the best players, the team statistics, the starting rotations, and so on. It seems to me that what I liked was being an "expert," the feeling that I had mastered the baseball card world.

As an adult I have noticed that whenever I feel I am becoming a "jack of all trades," that many things are done adequately and few done with mastery, my soul seems to wither. And so my remembering of baseball cards reminds me that mastery is my way in the world and it must be respected. Whenever I have respected my desire to "master" things, to go deeper than the surface and become an "expert," my soul engages.

Another important thing I remember about my childhood is how I always had a "best friend." This may be true for many children, but I remember not getting much satisfaction from "group" friendships. What made me most happy was having one or two great one-on-one friends. It was not until I was in my early forties that I realized how little energy I had put into nurturing really good one-on-one friendships in my adult years. The lack of these relationships in my life had impacted my spirit in ways that I never appreciated, never understood. So I literally made a list of all the acquaintances I had who were "prospects" to become one-on-one friends. I did not call them and tell them they were on my list, I simply started calling them more often and suggesting we get together. When I began again to pay attention to this important element of my "natural way," my spirit was lifted and I now have several very good one-on-one friends again.

In our seminars, the laughter is often contagious as people contemplate the things they loved to do as children. For example, a woman in her fifties volunteered: "When I was young I loved to play at being a doctor, but no one wants to play now."

But the tone gets more serious when we ask the next question: What do you notice about what you loved to do as a child compared with your life as an adult?

One woman succinctly summed it up: "When I was young I played a lot, spent a great deal of time outside, felt very creative, and spent a good deal of time with friends. Now, I rarely get outside, play nowhere near enough, don't feel very creative, and spend far less time with friends than I would like." Enough said.

The last question they ponder brings innocence back into the picture: "What did you leave behind from your childhood that should be brought back into your life?"

In my own exploration, I have discovered key hints from my childhood about my natural "loves," things that move me toward innocent joy—my love of sports, my need for close friends, my love of the outside, my interest in things political. And by incorporating these elements back into my adult life, much of my innocent love of life has returned.

What do you remember loving to do as a child? What do the things you loved to do tell you about your natural way in the world? What parts of yourself have been left behind? Is there a way to recapture that child who mastered baseball cards, the explorer who searched the rocks for fossils, the young kid who loved to climb trees?

Reclaiming the Parts We Left Behind

An anonymous poet once wrote: "I turned my head, only for a moment, and the moment became my life." When I consider those words, my response is visceral, emotional, and they cut me to the heart. We turn our heads, thinking it is only for a moment—and that moment becomes our entire life.

A woman once came up to me after a talk and shared her story with me. Her face said she was well into her forties, but her story told me she had come to a place where the poet's words would find resonance. "You know, when I took this job in government it was supposed to be temporary. That was twenty-three years ago. What happened to all those years? Now, before it's too late, I'm leaving," she told me.

"What will you do?" I inquired.

"I don't know," she answered, a sparkle in her eyes. "I guess I'll try to find those parts of myself that I left behind."

If we are to live with innocence all of our days, to see life again with fresh eyes, we must begin to believe that we can reclaim those childhood loves and inclinations. We must begin to put aside the adult we have become, the one that keeps telling us to grow up, to be practical, to pay attention to the things we "should" pay attention to.

So . . . what did you love to do when you were young?

4

Detours: They're Not What You Expect

"When you come to a fork in the road, take it."
— Yogi Berra

The best things in life are not in your day-timer and probably weren't on your ten-year goal list. Although we make plans incessantly, many of the things we look back on with fondness were never in the grand game plan of our life. Our lives often unfold in a myriad of ways that were never part of our well-laid plans. If we are to experience a second innocence in our lives, to reconnect with the joy and wonder of life, we must begin to rethink how we see detours, the inevitable forks in the road that life gives us. Our commitment to our plans can blind us to the very path our soul wants to take us.

When I was a young minister I had mapped out my entire career starting at age twenty-five. In orderly five-year chunks, I carefully laid out each step of my forty-year-long career and what I wanted to be doing in each of those time periods, ending when I was somewhere around 60 to 65 when I would finish my career as a wise and a revered seminary professor. It would be great fun to dig up that five-year increment plan today and look at it with the perspective of how my life has actually unfolded.

Ironically, that carefully crafted road map may have helped ensure my departure from the ministry. I had set a clear plan to go to a bigger church in a specific time frame and set my sights on making that plan a reality. When a dynamic (but small) church outside of San Antonio, Texas, asked me to move there as their leader, I turned them down (graciously, I hope). They simply were not large enough to fit my plan. Instead, six months later I took an assignment at a larger church in San Diego. The assignment was a disaster and I left the ministry in part because of it. Fortunately, my openness to detours thereafter led me to a great vocation and I have learned that a narrow focus on the "plan" has never served me well.

How many of us have taken a promotion, made a move, taken marriage vows, and so on, because we believed it to be the next step in our plan? And how many of us have missed opportunities for the renewal of our soul because it did not fit with the "map" for our life?

Too often in life we get an idea in our heads, and in the process close our hearts to the gentle nudging of the spirit to wander off the path. Innocence is possible only when we recognize that detours are neither good nor bad—they are simply signs and opportunities. Our tendency to judge detours as obstacles often blinds us to their hidden possibilities. Detours are intrinsic to the human experience in that every life is filled with unplanned twists and turns. And given how much these detours are part of the human experience, feeling the need to avoid them is quite stressful, if not counterproductive. Perhaps when a detour presents itself, our first response should be: "Isn't it interesting that I have come to this possibility? I wonder where it might lead."

What I Learned on My Drive to School

When I was a graduate student at Kent State University working on my Ph.D., I drove a particular route to school every day. It was a predictable, boring 45-minute ride through the cornfields and industrial areas of northeast Ohio. Each Tuesday and Thursday for almost a year I took this drive. One morning, running slightly late as always (at the time my nickname was "the late great John Izzo"), I ran smack into a "Road Closed" sign and an arrow pointing to the detour. For two weeks the main road would be closed. Turning left (and cussing the state, the county, and the rest of the world in the process), the road took me through rolling farmland to a "T" crossing. When I turned right and drove around a corner, there before me was one of the most beautiful ponds I have ever seen. It was June and the tiny lake was awash in vibrant greens, the water surrounded by large old trees. The sight of it took my breath away and I literally stopped on the side of the road for ten minutes to take in its beauty. For almost a year I had driven a monotonous journey through industrial neighborhoods while this lovely pond sat waiting for me. Two weeks later the detour sign came down, but I kept turning left.

For the last year of my time at Kent State, the detour became the main road and although it took an extra ten minutes I looked forward to the ride each morning. Summer gave way to a beautiful autumn of ever-changing colors and falling leaves reflected in the pond's still water. Winter arrived, first with a barren brownness, then giving way to a snowy wonderland and a frozen lake of pure white. Spring arrived with bursting buds of lovely lime-green that shone in the pond like an Impressionist painting and finally returned to the glorious deep summer-green that had greeted me the year before. The detour became more than a way to get to school; it became a teacher and a reminder of the beauty that surrounds us if we are only willing to stray off the path on which we are set.

How many times in our lives do we look back and curse the detours, the times when the promotion did not happen, when the relationships did not work out, the roads closed, the acceptance letters that never came—only to discover that those very detours led to wonderful experiences we would not have had should the main road have remained open?

Of course, not all detours lead to beautiful ponds. But any detour can offer us something new and unexpected. We can curse these detours or we can open our hearts to them. We can choose to accept them while grasping the possibilities or we can fight to stay on the main road. What detours has life thrown you lately and what plans do you have that may be blocking the new path?

Can't See the Forest for the Trees

This focus on the "planned road" robs life of its richness in the simplest of things. In the summer following my sophomore year in college at Hofstra University on Long Island, I took an assignment as a volunteer at a community center for inner city children in Chicago. Although I had never been more than 250 miles away from home on my own, I flew across the country to help others. Since I had some background in acting, I wound up being cast in a summer stock production of *Kiss Me, Kate* in suburban Chicago. The play is a wonderful musical with a large chorus so I was surrounded for weeks by a throng of people my own age, many of the opposite sex. I wanted very much to find love that summer.

The object of my desire was Kay, a beautiful young woman playing the lead role of the Shrew (this should have been my first clue—everyone's heard of typecasting). I focused on Kay with single-minded passion and there was much tension as I tried to win her. For weeks, being attached to that specific result, I was miserable, trying every which way to woo her. My affection for Kate was growing, and winning her was my "plan." However, as is often the case, life had other ideas.

Finally, halfway through the summer came word through a mutual friend that Kay was simply not interested. I was devastated. But, my friend indicated, there was another gal in the chorus, Lynn, and word had it that she liked me very much. Focused as I was on Kay, I had hardly noticed Lynn. But with my attention now turned— more present and less tense—what I noticed was a bright, bubbly, attractive, sensitive young woman whose curiosity about me was evident. It was not until I opened up to life instead of trying to control it that this wonderful detour opened up.

But to what problem does this simple summer interlude relate? My focus on Kay actually made me less present. Instead of being attentive and aware, my life became focused on a future goal: Would I win Kay or not? This attachment to a particular result (results ultimately out of my control) blinded me to other possibilities. Had I simply held out the intention to connect with others and stayed present I would likely have met Lynn weeks before. The four weeks we had together might have been eight weeks, and I regret my stubborn focus on the "plan."

This simple scenario is played out in our lives every day. We attach to results, we blind ourselves to other roads and wind up feeling miserable rather than at peace. Even worse, instead of waking up each day and enjoying the journey, we spend our days watching the dashboard.

This happens in big things as well. William Wordsworth, the great English writer and poet, had plans to write his life's work. But he had a feeling that there was something he had to get out of his system before he began his autobiography. He began to write a poem he titled *The Prelude*, so called because it would be the prelude to his true life's work. Ironically, *The Prelude*—a modern epic—is considered by many to be his most important work. *The Prelude* turned out to be the main event.

Make no mistake: It is not that we should go through life without plans or clear desires. But life is an organic creation, the serendipitous intersection of thousands of events that put us in a certain place at a certain time. Being closed to the many detours presented to us and allowing our life plans to shield us from other possibilities means we will ultimately enjoy a less than satisfying journey. Children are very good at this and it may help explain why they seem to be able to change plans at a moment's notice and engage with whatever activity is presented to them. Unfortunately, as we grow older, we become obsessed with planning our lives and experience deep disappointment when life does not follow our orderly expectations (which it inevitably does not).

This principle plays itself out even in the daily rhythm of life. We map out our daily life as I mapped out my five-year plans in such a way that we constantly miss opportunities to experience joy. As a simple example, some weeks ago I was feeling frustrated that my busy schedule had not allowed much time for friends. That Monday I had a packed schedule with little free time, ending in a board meeting that would go until 8 P.M. After the board meeting a friend and fellow board member asked what I was doing right then (the intimation being that perhaps we could have a beer and connect a bit). My immediate response was to think of my orderly plan for the day (board meeting over at eight, home by nine, in bed by half past ten in time for an early alarm bell so I could write the next morning). Here my day was offering me a detour squarely in the direction of the very intention I had set out that morning—to connect with friends. After a moment's hesitation I accepted the detour and had a great time. Now, for those who live an entirely spontaneous life, accepting detours readily and with a smile, this illustration may seem almost silly. But for those whose lives are planned out like a military intervention, you know what I'm talking about. As the Bible puts it: "Let them who have ears hear."

At a deeper level this is also about recognizing that we should focus on the overall direction of our life more than reaching a specific destination. This distinction is profoundly important. When we focus on creating certain "values" in our lives as opposed to certain "results," we are much happier. Finding a mate we love rather than one with the specific eight characteristics we envision; creating deep friendships but being open to who those people might be; taking on more responsibility in our careers but not obsessing about a particular position we aspire to—all these are simply an opening up of ourselves to the possibilities presented to us every day. Life is not packaged and neat. It has detours for us and when we are open to them they often become the main road.

The Path Less Traveled

This openness to detours also means that we do not wait for the perfect opportunity to get into the game. The brief half hour of connection with a friend is as invigorating as an all-day spa treatment. The short walk at the end of your day is as important as the carefully planned hike. We stop waiting for the perfect opportunity to get started and simply take the roads available to us.

Indeed, one of the ways we continue to fall in love with our lives and experience a sense of wonder is by being open to the dynamic process that weaves the tapestry of our life. So long as we keep heading in a direction, the direction of the leanings of our truest spirit, life has a way of falling into place.

The great stage actress Helen Hayes was interviewed in her later years and asked if she felt she had lived a happy life. After some moments of reflection she replied: "When you ask if I have had a happy life, I would say I have had many happy moments. It seems to me that when I think about my life, it is like a beautifully woven tapestry. If you get too close to it, all you see are fibers of color and thread. But somehow, if I could rise above, far enough to see the entire tapestry, I believe the threads have woven a beautiful pattern." The detours, guided by simple attention, had created a rich life. But each thread, each piece seen on its own, had not been exactly as she had planned.

So take life on its terms and allow the tapestry to unfold. The detour sign in front of you may be pointing to the main road; that "prelude" you are working on may wind up being your life's work. The person you want to love you so much may be standing next to the person who could make your dreams come true. I have learned that life has its own rhythm and is lived best with an open heart. And one more thing I've learned: You really never know if a detour is fortune or misfortune until a long time after it occurs.

In 1995 I was vice-president at a consulting company, living someone else's life. Driven by my need for security and status, my plan was to stay at the company for five more years, build up a financial nest egg, and then start my own business. The company experienced a hostile takeover: The president (my boss) was fired and I was handed a contract with which I could not live. I quit and they withheld my bonus, a large sum of money I had fully earned. The weekend this occurred I was deeply depressed and my well-laid plans seemed to have hit a gigantic "Road Closed" sign. To this day I can remember conducting a retreat for a large health care client in the Southern California desert knowing I would not be paid for my work and wondering why life had dealt me this unfortunate blow to my career plans.

Turns out the detour meant that I gained much sympathy from most of my large clients. They all gave me their business, including one who happened to employ my future wife as a manager. Another CEO, the one at the retreat I did for nothing after quitting, gave me a two-year contract to "help me get my business going." The detour forced me out into the world on my own and I wrote my first book, *Awakening Corporate Soul*, as I struggled with my own experience of corporate insensitivity. That book led me to start working with leaders on creating a deeper path, one aligned with my work in ministry. I can't be sure, but I believe this "Road Closed" sign led me to write my first book, helped me start a career I love, and is the reason I met the woman with whom I have made a wonderful life.

We often say: "life is funny." Perhaps what we really mean is that it isn't orderly. You never know what might happen, but next time a detour comes, put your report card away, take a drive and keep your eyes open for the beautiful pond that might lie just around the next corner.

5

It's a Great Life If You Don't Weaken

Approaching my grandmother's hospital room, I was suddenly taken by the enormity of the news about to be delivered. I have made a life of words, written and spoken, but there are no good words for what I must say.

Just arriving from a four-hour cross-country flight, I had been chosen for this task because I was a minister, because I was a writer and work with words, because, even more than my mother, this is the woman who raised me. And because, most of all, no one else wants to be the one to do this!

Entering the door of the hospital room, the smell of sickness overwhelmed my senses. The smell was familiar from my days in the ministry—the unmistakable air of every hospital room. My thoughts went back to hospital visits when I was the "preacher" with the duty of bringing hope into rooms such as this. It took me years to realize that I brought only my love and my concern, and that—luckily—those two things were usually enough. The older I get, the less I say to someone in grief and the more I try simply to be present.

On one such visit, there was Barney with the inoperable tumor. By the time I visited him the tumor was the size of a grapefruit, but he still had his sense of humor. Then there was the man whose wife had died in an accident in which he was the driver (and at fault); the man whose injury would paralyze him for life; and a myriad of elderly souls who were ready to take the final journey.

There were amusing times as well, such as the time I visited Ellen, a blind woman with diabetes. While I was there, they had to change her IV line. It did not go well and blood was spurting all over the floor and bed. Ellen was fine, but the young clergyman was passed out on the floor with three nurses trying to revive him. Thank goodness the woman is blind, I thought, no one will ever have to know. My hopes for anonymity were erased the next Sunday morning when her uncle Will, a farmer and great kidder, shook my hand at the end of the service and I felt something in his hand. Smelling salts! His whole family cracked up with joyous laughter.

All of those times visiting my flock, the words had somehow found me. I prayed they would find me now.

My grandmother was sitting up in her bed when I walked in and she seemed both surprised and elated to see me. A broken hip had placed her in the bed, but she knew a broken hip was not enough of a reason to call her busy grandson from California to her bedside in New York.

As if she knew there was a shoe to drop, we sat for a moment in silence holding each other's hand. "Nanna," I said, "I have some bad news to give you." Swallowing hard, looking into her eyes, the words came out: "Nanna, Shirley . . . well, Nanna, she's dead. Yesterday she jumped off the Bayonne Bridge. She didn't survive and it's in all the papers today." Shirley was her oldest daughter, and my aunt.

For what seemed like an eternity, she sat in silence, tears running down her face. She had endured the Depression, the early death of her only true love, the divorces of all three of her daughters, the deaths of her parents, and now this. She looked at me: "John, it takes a great deal of courage to live. Shirley, the poor girl, she never had much of that." The words were spoken with no cruelty, but with the loving knowledge that only a mother can have.

I have never forgotten those words of my grandmother: "It takes courage to live." I have come to realize that it does *not* take a great deal of courage to get through life, merely to gut it out. But to live one's whole life in the innocence of our youth, holding on to our ideals, moving on through the inevitable hardships and disappointments, living one's convictions, to be a person of faith in a world where people become cynical and jaded, to believe that peace is possible when everyone else has given up—all of these things take a great deal of courage.

Courage is an interesting word. We often think of courage as a willingness to risk great danger, to face risks and not waver. We speak of war heroes, explorers, and adventurers as having a good deal of courage. The word actually derives from the Old English word for *heart*. It is defined as the "quality of mind which enables one to encounter danger and difficulties with firmness, or without fear, or fainting of heart." The connection between "heart" and courage has become clear to me throughout my life. My courage has been most evident and easy to access when my heart has been most convicted and committed. Another way of thinking of this is that when our heart is deeply committed to something, courage comes naturally. So the great challenge for living a courageous life is to discover and claim the things to which your heart is most committed, for it is when we are attached to those things that courage will find us. Courage is also a choice not to lose heart in spite of the disappointments and the loss of ideals that are all too often a part of adult life.

Herein is the key point, the one my grandmother tried to teach me that day, sitting as she was like a frail bird on the edge of her hospital bed, eighty years of hardship and joy behind her—it takes courage not to lose heart and losing heart is a choice.

Courage is a choice we make each moment of our lives, a choice to hold on to our ideals, to continue to affirm life and its purpose, to believe in love however much it has failed us, and to believe in the ultimate purpose of our good deeds even when evil appears to be winning.

Yes, you ask, and rightly so, but where does courage come from? It is a posture we decide to take in the world. It is not simply some gene in our DNA, one that—like the cowardly lion—we can say we were born without. It is in each of us, waiting to be awakened at the moment of need.

If we believe courage is a trait that others have that we cannot access, then we give ourselves permission to lose heart and let go of our ideals. We can say then that we admire those courageous people who stay the course, live their convictions, love in spite of hurt—but we are not able to do that. Courage is a choice, one that is made again and again in our lives.

When I was young, my grandmother used to have a saying, one she used when things were tough. I must have heard it hundreds of times: "It's a great life if you don't weaken." And it is easy to weaken, to lose heart, unless we choose to be innocent again and open up to life's possibilities.

In what area of life are you tempted to weaken? In what realms right now is courage required to hold on to your ideals, to take the risk of love and goodness in spite of risk?

Six years after that day in the hospital room, my grandmother was diagnosed with lung cancer. Mercifully, she had a very brief illness and died within two weeks. She had lived with my mother for many years and it always seemed to me that there was a great silence between them. They loved each other, if love is judged by actions and not by the words, but I could never recall truly warm words between them. For all my grandmother's courage, she was never a very expressive woman. Her friends used to tell me how proud she was of me and that she bragged about me all the time, yet she would rarely say such things to me in person. My mother, her youngest daughter, went to the hospital to collect her things. In her purse, Nanna had penned a brief note to my mother: "Irene, I know I was a burden for many years, but thank you for taking care of me. You were, you know, always my favorite."

Sure, my grandmother should have said all that sooner, should have had the courage and heart to say it long before. But it is never too late to be courageous.

6

Mr. Thom's Lesson:
Living Our Ideals

It was seventh grade and I was just starting junior high school at Intermediate School 27 in New York City. It took about a week to figure out that going to this school was not going to be a fun experience.

The first week at lunch the ordeal began. The older and tougher kids started hitting me up for money. It was not much really, a nickel here and a dime there, enough to buy a snack or two. And it was not the money that got to me; rather, it was the daily humiliation and the almost constant fear. To know each day that someone will threaten you eats away at the spirit. Leaving school, I had been beaten up several times, nothing too serious and not for money—just for the fun of it.

I tried not to tell my mother about it. She was a single mother, working hard to make ends meet. She needed no more burdens. (My son, Carter, gets bullied too when he is in fifth grade and it is hard for him to tell us. He is not short like I was, but he is sensitive and it occurs to me that perhaps schools were not meant for sensitive kids. He will outgrow it all, but for now my heart breaks; his feelings are familiar to me.)

The school had hundreds of students and the scores of teachers. The most admired teachers were the gym teachers, tough, jocular men who ruled their classes like drill sergeants and who sent us up the ropes with loud barks. If you are ever in trouble, call a gym teacher, I thought.

Then there was Mr. Thom, a short guy with bushy brown hair, thick glasses, and a slightly squeaky voice. He taught math (naturally) and, try as he might, he could not control those tough inner city kids. No one respected Mr. Thom and kids made fun of him frequently. His class was a three-ring circus of misbehavior.

One day in the cafeteria, the place of least supervision, an eighth grader who was already more than six feet tall got involved with a custodian in a verbal confrontation that turned violent. The student grabbed a metal scraper from the custodian's work belt. Within moments, the man's face was bleeding as the student scraped and slashed the custodian. The kid showed no sign of stopping.

The students circled around, gawking like spectators in the Roman Coliseum. Some chanted, some cheered, others stared in disbelief, many—I hoped—were thinking what I was thinking: "Someone help this poor man." There were many teachers standing around, including two of the gym teachers. But they simply watched in silence. No one interfered; the blood was getting more profuse and started to puddle on the floor.

Out of nowhere a small man broke through the crowd, plaid sport coat, mismatched tie, floppy hair, and all. He jumped on the back of the six-foot student and rode him like a bucking bronco at the rodeo. He couldn't stop him and was jerked around on the young brute's back like a doll, but still he bear-hugged him with all his strength, holding on for dear life—not his, but the custodian's. With all the strength he could muster, he pulled the kid from the custodian and they fell together to the floor. Now that it was safe, the gym teachers joined in and finally the bloodbath stopped, just short of death. Shaken but resolute, Mr. Thom brushed his hair away from his face. There was blood on his chin and on his hands.

Over the next few weeks, Mr. Thom did not become a folk hero. The kids still acted up in his class, yet all but the worst among us began to see him differently. Somehow we knew now that underneath his quiet, droopy demeanor was a person of great courage. When the moment to live his values presented itself, he did not flinch or keep himself out of harm's way.

Over the next few weeks the gym teachers still barked their commands for us to climb the ropes but somehow with less enthusiasm. They would never admit it but they knew that when their time came to show what they were truly made of, they had been unprepared. And who could blame them really: a wild, half-insane student swinging a blade with reckless abandon. How many of us would have done what Mr. Thom did?

Maybe that is the real point of what happened in the cafeteria. Second innocence is about reclaiming our ideals, grabbing hold of our convictions again, even if we surprise ourselves in the process. I can't be certain, but even as a young idealistic teenager I had this sense that Mr. Thom's soul—like the Grinch's heart—grew a few sizes larger that day. It grew because he had reclaimed a part of himself he may have forgotten existed. And it is in those moments, when we have a chance again to claim our ideals, that the purpose of life is renewed. The opposite is also true, that a part of our innocence dies each time we fail to live up to our own ideals.

I think of some of my own moments. The time when I was a young minister and members of my church board were telling jokes about "niggers" and "porch monkeys" before the meeting of the church board. I wanted so much to speak up angrily, to turn over the table like Jesus throwing out the money handlers in the temple. The words were right there and ready to come out, but my mouth moved without saying a word. It seems to me that I died a little bit in that meeting.

Then there was the time my wife discovered a deceit I had held from her. For months there were literally hundreds of times when the words were almost out of my mouth, where telling her the truth and claiming my ideal of honesty was right there, but courage eluded me. To this day the regret of having been found out as opposed to the courage of being forthright haunts me. It probably always will.

There have, of course, been moments when I did lay it on the line, gave it all that there was to give, uncertain of the results. Though these opportunities may be few and far between, they are to be cherished, for to experience them and be up to the task is a part of what it means to be fully human.

Somehow I think the true test of leadership and of living is how we hold to our convictions when it isn't easy. Anyone can tell the truth when there are no consequences; but put us in a moment when the truth could embarrass us or worse and the true mettle of a person emerges. Speaking up when everyone is angry about an injustice is important, but if you want to live a truly extraordinary life, speak up when everyone else is silent and you know some feathers will be ruffled by what you dare say. And I am the first to admit there aren't many of those moments—which is precisely why they mean so much when they do come.

In my moments of truth, the moments when I have the rare chance to truly claim my ideals, I try to remember Mr. Thom. I try to hold his image in my mind, his flailing, flopping hair flying everywhere in the fray, David on the back of Goliath, the moment when life gave him a chance to fully live his convictions and he said yes.

7

Reclaiming Awe
and Wonder

As my daughter voraciously read through the Harry Potter books, it occurred to me that innocence has much to do with two simple words: awe and wonder. Children seem able to find this wonder in the simplest of things—an unusual bug on the sidewalk, a puddle that is particularly deep, a small paper airplane.

As we age, somehow our capacity for awe and wonder is diminished, just as our skin loses its elasticity. Years of smiling (or frowning) create lines in the face that at some point defy erasing or even cosmetic injections. In the same way, it is possible to create wrinkle lines in the soul that diminish our capacity to embrace the moments of wonder that animate life so wonderfully.

So how do we recapture the experience of wonder? We begin by remembering those moments when we have had such experiences, when the wonder of life touched us, not in our conscious, linear mind, but in some deeper place. For many of us, nature is one of the best sources of rekindling this sense of wonder—yet we have so little of it in our lives, trapped as we are by habit and necessity in offices and schools. For me, these mystical moments in touch with nature are the things I remember most about being alive.

Earlier this year we moved into a new house. Our old home was like a tree house, nestled in a cedar forest, overlooking the sea and mountains from the vantage point of the birds. In our new home we are much closer to the water. We had been there for a few weeks and it was summer; the nights were very warm, so we were sleeping with the windows wide open. One night, I woke up and could not get back to sleep. There was a sound outside my window that was unfamiliar to me, a sound like people walking over gravel. There are railroad tracks behind our house, so my mind wondered who might be walking on the tracks at 3 A.M.. and for some time I lay there listening until I could not help but look.

Going over to the window I sat down and gazed out into the night, but there was no one on the tracks. Yet the sound continued. It took me a while, but I figured out that what I was hearing was the sound of small waves lapping against the shoreline 50 yards from our house. With the sound of the waves lapping, I saw that it was a perfectly clear night, hundreds of stars dancing in the crisp air, with the mountains on the other side of the sound a more solid contrast. For an hour, I simply sat on the floor looking out my window and listening to the waves. Now and then, it occurred to me that I would be tired in the morning, but I did not want this moment to end. Finally, I went back to bed and slept the sleep of the contented. The next night I tried again for this feeling of awe but couldn't hear the waves and went to back to bed. And as I lay quietly, eyes closed, that moment of awe and wonder returned. It had not left me. I can recapture the innocence of the moment whenever I wish.

Since so many of my times of wonder and those of others mentioned to me have been connected to nature, it seems that spending more time in the natural world, even briefly, can profoundly animate our days.

But can awe and wonder carry us through the harsher realities of life? Will these moments carry me forward when death and suffering surround me? Are moments of wonder enough?

Wonder Can Break Through the Hard Stuff

Most of John's life had been spent outdoors, hiking in wilderness and living adventurously. Now, in his 50s, he had been lying for six weeks in a hospital bed, dying of brain cancer. Friends and family were on a 24-hour deathwatch, taking turns at his bedside so that when the time came—and it would come soon—someone he loved would be there. His friend Bryan did not like to see him lying there, staring at the sterile walls of his hospital room; he knew it must have been withering his soul to have stopped having the "moments." So one day he asked John if he wanted to go outside. John's face lit up. Of course he would like to go outside. It took some doing, but Bryan convinced the nurses to use a small crane to move him from bed and get him into a wheelchair. After zipping John inside a sleeping bag, off went the pair in a taxi equipped for the disabled, heading to the mountains just north of the city. As they arrived in the mountains, it began to rain. It was not a gentle rain, but an all-out gully washer, the kind of downpour for which Vancouver is famous.

Do you remember when rain was not something to shield yourself from? As a young child I remember coming home from elementary school one day in a pouring rainstorm. To this day I can recall the feeling of being drenched by the warm rain, splashing in every puddle until I was soaking wet, smiling every step of the way home as claps of thunder ignited our path. Long before the message about catching one's "death of cold" or "being practical" had sunk in, rain was something to be felt and experienced. At some point, rain became something else: the cancellation of the picnic, the end of the baseball game, a nuisance. Rain—the very thing that brings life to the planet—ceased to be an experience of wonder and became something simply to be endured.

Standing at the side of the taxi, my friend Bryan held the umbrella over the wheelchair, looking down at his friend whose mind was still present, but whose body was quickly leaving him. Bryan asked: "John, it's not a very good day. Are you sure you want to do this?"

After a moment's pause, John replied, "Bryan, it would be a very good day, a very good day indeed, if you would just put that umbrella down for a few moments and let that rain fall on my face."

Reluctantly Bryan folded the umbrella and his friend turned his face up to the sky, the tactile feeling of the great outdoors once again (and literally) washing over him. His face broke into a broad smile. It was indeed a good day. Even in the face of the harshest truth, awe and wonder have a way of breaking through. In fact, sometimes it takes a cancer, an illness, a wake-up call, to remind us of what we knew as children: that rain can be sweet and gentle, that life is there waiting for us at those moments when we choose to be—as e. e. cummings wrote—"glad and young" again.[1]

In his book *Living Buddha, Living Christ*, Thich Nhat Hanh writes: "If I am ever in an airplane and the pilot announces that our plane is about to crash, I will practice mindful breathing and take refuge in the island of the self. I know it is the best thing I can do."[2] I fly a good deal and have thought about that same question: What would I do? Breathing and mindfulness are very important, for only when we are awake and present can awe and wonder break through and remind us of what our hearts already know.

Yet if I am ever in that moment or something like it, when I know my seconds are few and running out fast, I believe I would try to remember those moments of awe and wonder—the wind that will blow forever, the stream that was rushing over my hand, the night the waves and stars joined together in a symphony outside my window, the day Steve and I were surrounded by the gloriously setting sun, the feeling of raindrops hitting my face in a Puerto Rican rain forest. I will hope that in remembering those moments, my innocent faith will speak to me of the things my mind cannot know.

How do we cultivate the experience of awe and wonder in our lives? It begins by keeping our eyes open, by being willing to stop in the middle of "important" stuff to breathe in the "little things." So perhaps awe and wonder are not things to behold but a posture we take, a choice to see the mystery that is alive in the universe.

One day, when my daughter Sydney was very young she interrupted me as I worked on a client report in my home office. She came to tell me "there is a beautiful and amazing bug just outside on the driveway. She is red and black and spotted. You must come see this bug."

Busy writing my report, I told her that the bug would have to wait. "Perhaps it'll be there when I'm done," I added. Sydney frowned but was undaunted.

"No, daddy," she said, "bugs do not wait for us." Awakened by her native wisdom, I joined her and we went down the long driveway to view the brightly colored caterpillar. Sure enough, the bug was amazing—black, red, spotted all over. For a few minutes, she and I shared in the absolute delight that God, evolution, or something greater than us had created such a lovely creature. Years later, I cannot recall a word from the report, nor even what report I was working on, but if I close my eyes I can still see that beautiful bug!

One does not have to live near the sea or in the mountains, have the perfect job or perfect spouse, to find this awe and wonder. We simply need to keep our eyes and senses open.

And yes, innocence and joy are almost always waiting just outside that window.

8

What Trees Can Teach Us

Nature is a great teacher. Its natural cycles demonstrate important truths about life and renewal, and this is why many of the great myths incorporate nature's imagery. I find trees to be great teachers. Every year, deciduous trees must drop their leaves so that new life can form. If the leaves did not fall, the tree could not renew itself. It is that simple. What can this cycle teach us about reclaiming our innocence, about rediscovering the wonder of life? I believe it teaches us that we pay too little attention to the role letting go plays in the experience of renewal.

While I was in the seminary in 1981 I spent some time in the Middle East. While our base was in Egypt, we also traveled to Israel and the Palestinian West Bank. We arrived after a period of riots and unrest in Ramallah and nearby towns. Coming from a young culture in North America I could not appreciate the historical perspective of those who lived in this place. People spoke to me of hurts thousands of years old, of lands stolen and people displaced. They spoke of soldiers with guns, of dead brothers and fathers, and most of all of the need to "never forget." Never forget the Holocaust; never forget the war of 1967; on and on it went. Somehow even to a naïve observer it was obvious that there would need to be much letting go for healing ever to be possible.

I use this example deliberately, because letting go often involves the releasing of hard things, of painful truths, of things that we may believe are best remembered. But nature reminds us that we cannot hold on forever. Only with letting go can new life come.

This takes many forms in our personal lives. When I was young, one of my uncles was a white-collar traveling salesman. In those days, the early '60s, salesmen drove their cars rather than hopping planes and he would frequently stop by our home on one of his sales trips.

As a young boy, these visits from Uncle Clayton were a pleasant surprise and something of an adventure. Because we were lower-middle class, I never got to meet many people outside the confines of my neighborhood, so having this distant uncle with the suit and brimmed hat bring a different world to our house—if only for a few hours—was always a highlight. He would arrive in his big white Cadillac, always unexpectedly, and sit at our kitchen table sipping coffee and making small talk. For a young boy in a blue-collar home whose father had died young, these visits were fascinating.

Then, when I was about nine years old, my great-grandmother died. She had been my favorite. As an adult I was told about her grumpy and sometimes mean temperament, but to me she was a saint who spent hours indulging me with the most precious gift, her time. I was not old enough for funerals, so my family went off to Connecticut to lay great-grandmother to rest while I remained behind.

Soon after her death, those wonderful visits from Uncle Clayton stopped, as did our occasional visits to his home in the country. It was not until many years later that I learned why.

When my great-grandmother died, there was a family feud

over her "stuff." My mother felt Uncle Clayton had cheated her mother out of a part of her rightful inheritance. Of course, he saw it differently; he felt that he had taken care of my great-grandmother for years, living in the same city and bearing the burden of doing so. Taking more of the things she left seemed appropriate. Turns out she did not have all that much anyway, but the consequences of those things being distributed in this way lasted forever. No one was willing to let go, to move on and allow new life to sprout. We never did get another visit nor did we ever visit again.

I cried when my uncle died many years later; I cried because that pain had not been let go. Winter had lasted forever and spring had never come. He never visited again nor was he welcome in our home.

The Power of Letting Go

In one of my seminars, a woman confessed she had been estranged from her son for more than thirty years. During the session we discussed the critical role that letting go plays in keeping ourselves from becoming cynical. Later that very day, this woman called her son. All the years of estrangement, years of hurt compounded and earning interest, were forgiven on both sides in a few moments. It was as if both had been waiting for someone to simply have the courage to loosen up and let go of the past. In the weeks that followed she told colleagues at work how she had begun to let go of her negativity, to let go of her blame toward others, to let go of her need to be right. It was as if by letting go in one area of her life, an avalanche of things that needed to be free had been shaken loose. Like one of our Pacific Northwest windstorms that remove all of fall's grandeur in a single afternoon, she had finally been liberated.

So autumn always makes me wonder what I am holding on to. What is it that I am afraid to let go of? One of the wonderful exercises of autumn is to spend time reflecting on a simple question: What is it that I need to release? What must be put aside so that spring can arrive?

Unclenching That Fist

About seven years ago I realized that I wanted to do different kinds of work with people and with organizations. My years of ministry seemed a distant memory and my work life had taken on the focus of helping leaders become more efficient and effective. I wanted to reclaim things of the spirit, but had built a very good life for myself as a consultant.

At about that time the book *Awakening Corporate Soul* had begun to germinate in me, but there was fear as well. At the time I thought it was fear about where the work would take me, but now I see it was mostly about what I'd have to leave behind. I had come to be seen as an expert in the arena of customer service; I was much in demand and making a good living. Perhaps a book on soul would pigeonhole me as "soft," removed from the real, daily concerns of clients. Perhaps if my shingle read "soul," the phone would stop ringing and for at least a time my image of myself as an expert would have to be modified to that of novice.

In one important moment, my colleague and old friend Tom Diamond said it all: "John, until you are willing to be a novice again, perhaps you cannot make this transition." That is, unless there was some letting go, the seasons could not take their natural turn.

That experience did lead to winter, moments wondering if the phone would ever ring again, moments feeling far too much like a novice, moments when the letting go seemed too much. But ever since that period, I have a much deeper respect for the place of letting go in moving forward.

My mother and I have been going through such a process. As

this book is being written we are making plans for her to move to our community from her lifetime home in New York City. After 65 years there, she will join us this summer to live out what we hope are many good years. Yet for almost 20 years she and I have been far from close. Mind you, unlike some families, we have not been at odds. We have not gone through any period when we refused to talk to each other or chose to ignore the other.

Rather, we went through two decades of holding on to moments from the past.

For my part, there were childhood hurts, ways my mother had raised me that had "wounded" me, things that had contributed to some of my many adult character flaws and helped explain my several failed relationships. Holding on to my need to blame someone and my wish that she had lived a different life kept me from being close to her. She, on the other hand, held on to the need to be the good mother, to see me as the fallen son who did not care about her.

Perhaps more than any hurt, we both had to let go of the idea that we must completely like each other. Somehow, when we finally let go of that need, we could simply love each other as mother and son—to put whatever hurt there had been behind us and let spring arrive. Like the woman attending my seminar, I learned how easy it was in the end to let it go. I have missed my mother all these years and she has undoubtedly missed me more deeply than my heart will let me take in.

What about for you? What image of yourself must be let go to allow a new image to form? What hurt do you hold very closely—yet the mere uncurling of fingers would gently release it? What way of being in the world must be allowed to fall for you to evolve as a human being? What part of your life must be "put aside" to make room for the deeper yearnings of your heart? What must be erased from the day-timer to allow other priorities to take hold? What opinions about the world and others keep you moving toward cynicism—and are you willing to let them go?

PART II

Rediscovering
the
Joy of Work

There is an old story in
the Zen tradition about Master Hyakujo.
Each day he would join his students for a period of
working. As the Master aged, his students felt it was inap-
propriate for him to subject himself to such labors. They
spoke with him, but their suggestion was brushed aside. One
monk took the matter into his own hands and hid the Master's tools.
The Master spent the next day in his room, sitting quietly. When the
attendant brought him his meals, Hyakujo nodded politely but took no
food. He simply sat. After three days of delivering food that was never
touched, the attendant pleaded, "Master, why do you not eat?"

Hyakujo replied: "A day of no work is a day of no eating!"

Work is a critical part of our identity as human beings and this may
help explain why up to 60 percent of us say we want to work, at least part-
time, until we are physically unable to do so. We also spend an inordinate amount of our time at work, as much as two-thirds of our waking lives. We even have a term for those who have lost their
innocence at work: burned out. But rediscovering our innocence in the realm of work is less about avoiding
burnout than it is about reclaiming the joy of
achievement and the belief that what we
do matters.

This next section is for all of us, whether we have a "career" or not. Our work in the world is more than what we do for a living, the role we play in or out of an organization. It is an expression of what we want to accomplish in the world before we die—in our workplaces, our families, and our communities.

In this section, through some of my most memorable experiences, I explore the opportunity to reclaim our innocence in work. As in most of sections in this book, you will discover truths about life as well as work. The last chapter in this section, *The Leader's Choice*, tells an important tale from my first experience of being a leader at work. This one chapter is specifically for leaders, but I suspect all readers will be amused by my experience and learn some truths about life in the process.

9

Your Job Is Bigger
Than You Think

"There are no great acts, only small acts performed with great love."
—Mother Teresa

It was the first week of my first year in graduate school. I had arrived in Chicago to study for the Presbyterian ministry and it was the middle of the year. Aware that I must work to fund my studies, I searched for a nice "save-the-world" part-time job, only to discover that all these had already been taken. No work in hospitals, social service agencies, anti-nuke organizations—nothing.

My new neighbors were a nice young couple from Wisconsin. Joe Hughes was studying for the Lutheran ministry and working part-time as a postal clerk in a small substation within a drug store on the south side of Chicago. In the middle of one of the poorest neighborhoods in the richest country in the world, Joe peddled stamps for 20 hours each week. "It doesn't pay all that well," Joe admitted, "but it is steady work and I enjoy it. If you want, I could put in a good word for you."

So he did, and a week later I started my six-month tenure as a postal clerk. Within a week my enthusiasm for the new job was history. For 20 hours each week, for the rest of the year, the young, would-be savior of the world licked stamps, printed money orders, and weighed packages. Yuck!

By the end of the first month I hated the job and didn't like the customers much, either. Peggy, who owned and ran the drug store, was a crabby old penny-pincher. Little things started to drive me bananas, like writing money orders. People came in and asked for ten money orders and I, from my middle-class background, wondered if poor people in Chicago had ever heard of checking accounts. I longed to do "important work" but, each week, this was my fate: a young idealist, out to make a difference, working in a post office. As the weeks went by, I found myself becoming more and more grumpy—and it showed. Who cares, I asked myself. When I get one of those save-the-world jobs they'll see what I'm made of.

Now Joe seemed to be having a different experience, but since we worked different shifts I had no clue what he saw in the work. As summer approached, I feared I would find myself working full-time in the postal substation. Just a few short weeks later, a letter arrived informing me of my acceptance as director of a boy's camp. I was thrilled beyond belief: finally work worthy of a young future star. No more stamps, no more packages, no more money orders—and no more Peggy.

Having informed her of my imminent departure, I was working the first of my last five shifts. It was a rainy Chicago day at the end of May and the fourth customer in line was an elderly black woman well into her eighties. She was short and wore a brimmed hat. The raindrops dripped onto her shoulders as she asked for a money order.

"How are you today?" I inquired distractedly.

She frowned. "Oh son, I am not well today. My daughter is in the hospital, she has cancer. The doctors told me yesterday that she is going to die, maybe today, maybe tomorrow, any time now. And I should be there, sitting by her side, but if I don't pay my rent by 5 P.M. today they'll evict me. And those lousy people who own the building won't let you pay in cash." She paused and then said, "But, for God's sake, I should be there, by her side. She's dying as we speak."

Some twenty-five years later, I cannot recall the specific words I said to her that day. I do know that for the first time in six months it occurred to me that I might actually have made a difference in the post office. After an exchange of kind and tender words she headed off, but at the door she stopped and turned around. Stepping back to my counter, putting her shaking, small, feeble hand on my young forearm, she looked deeply into my eyes: "Son, I just want to thank you. Thank you for being so kind. You do know, you made my day!"

That night sleep would not come. Her words kept ringing in my ears: "You made my day." For months I had seen my job at the post office as licking stamps and weighing things. Could it be that during that time there had been a deeper calling? What would have happened if I had thought about my job in that dingy, dark drugstore as "making people's days"?

The next morning at the post office I wrote these words down: "Make someone's day!" The first woman in line was another little old lady, wearing a bright orange dress. As she fumbled with her stamps I commented about how beautiful she looked in that fine dress.

After looking around and noticing there were only men nearby, she blushed. "Oh, go on," she said, but I knew I had made her day. No more parents with dying daughters were in my line that week, but in small and gentle ways my words and actions began to brighten the often-hard lives of my customers, even if it was for just a moment.

REDISCOVERING THE JOY OF WORK

As fate had it, Joe Hughes and I finished our work at the post office the same week. My leaving was hardly noticed, but the customers threw a going-away party for Joe on his last shift. By then I knew why. For Joe, the post office was a part of his ministry. He knew that wherever people were gathered, whatever your job description said you were supposed to be doing, you were there to make lives better—and it showed. The job was not too small for me; I was too small for the job.

Our Jobs Are Bigger Than We Are

I have never forgotten that job, though it has taken me years to truly embrace its lessons. Our jobs are almost always bigger than we are. And one of the keys to staying in love with our work is to continue to see the wonder available to us at work, to always see the noble possibilities in our role. One manager sees his job as making the payroll; another sees herself as mentoring young people. A bellman at a hotel thinks of his job as moving bags; another sees himself as making people feel at home. A gardener sees her job as pulling weeds; another thinks about the smile people will have when they pass by and see only beautiful flowers. A receptionist sees her job as answering the phone; another believes she can brighten the lives of people with her voice. And so it goes.

It is worth reflecting on the way you see your work right now. Are you licking stamps or making people's days? Are you making payroll or mentoring people? Moving bags or making people feel at home? Selling cars or helping someone find a car they will love so much they'll give it a name?

Years later, I would discover that a large part of leadership is to help others see the deeper possibilities in their roles. For some time I had an assistant named Susan and one week I called from the road to check in at the office. She sounded grumpy and a bit down. When

I asked how she was, she told me that this week she was stuffing 5,000 envelopes to promote my book *Awakening Corporate Soul* and that it was not a very soulful task. Listening to her, I could see myself standing there in the post office, about her age, moaning about licking stamps and mailing envelopes.

"Susan," I said with sincerity, "stuffing envelopes isn't a great deal of fun. But somewhere in those envelopes is the name of someone who will read this book and it will change her life. It will lead her to make a very important decision that will impact her fate and those around her. You are not stuffing envelopes—you are changing lives." She grunted and handed me off to our marketing director.

When I returned on Friday, I noticed that on the wall she had changed a sign from "Books Sold" to "Lives Changed." And, she confessed to me, about halfway through the week she started believing it, that her job had become bigger, and the innocent belief in the power of a stuffed envelope had turned a mundane task into holy work.

How do we fall in love with our work? I think we must never forget that we are always on holy ground if our eyes are open. We must never stop looking with innocent wonder at what our jobs might produce if we bring more of ourselves to them.

When Lloyd Hill became the CEO of Applebee's Restaurants he had just finished a stint in health-care management. Although he enjoyed his new work at Applebee's, he missed the deep sense of purpose he had discovered in health care where they were "changing lives" every day. But as he spent time out in the restaurants he noticed that in some of the restaurants people left a little better than when they came in. This was usually the result of small acts performed by people with big hearts: the waitress who remembered your name or favorite food, the smile and friendly chatter of the person who seated you, or simply the positive energy that flowed from staff people. Lloyd then realized that the work they were doing was bigger than he had thought, that his restaurant chain existed not just to serve food but to make every customer's life just a little better for having spent time there. Over the years he has shared that perspective with many people and admits that a few people glaze over when he does so, but also that many people begin to have a different experience at work when their job gets bigger, when licking stamps becomes making someone's day.

My mother was a manager for many years at one of the world's largest accounting firms. When she retired (the first time), she took a job as a receptionist at a research institute for the mentally challenged and it felt like quite a demotion. Her first day on the job someone asked her a question and she responded "How would I know? I am only a receptionist." The person looked her square in the eyes: "Only a receptionist! You are the first person people see and talk to when they come in here. How you treat them will send them a message about the entire organization and what it stands for. If you do your job well, that first message will be that we care." My mother realized in that moment that she was not "a" receptionist, she was "the" receptionist, an ambassador for an entire institute.

In my first real shot at acting, I had a very small part as a servant holding a torch in *Romeo and Juliet* at Hofstra University's Globe stage. Three hours every night, for four weeks, I sat through the entire play to hold my torch and say my one line: "Who goes there?" Mr. Van Werth, the director, told me that old cliché: "There are no small parts, only small actors." I did not believe him and told him so. After my year at the post office, I sent him a note to tell him he was right—if not about acting, then about life.

Is it possible that whatever you are doing, your true work is nobler than you think? When we see the possibilities in each moment, when we reflect on how we can save the world a little bit in every interaction we have and in every role we play, life changes in wonderful and mysterious ways.

10

What's Wrong with Rose-Colored Glasses?

We are all familiar with the old saying "He sees the world through rose-colored glasses." Usually meant as an insult, it is a way of saying that someone is a bit too innocent, that he or she sees the world with too much optimism. The intimation is straightforward: Wake up and smell the coffee.

Some people see the world through other kinds of glasses—cynical glasses—and surely the lenses they choose color their experiences. When it comes to rediscovering wonder and innocence at work, few decisions are more critical than choosing your glasses.

My son, Carter, had a teacher in third grade named Mrs. Smith (not her real name). Two months into the school year we were called to her office for a "problem-student" parent-teacher conference. Our son had been missing homework assignments and performing poorly on tests. We were prepared to hear about all of his character flaws, most of which he undoubtedly inherited.

Halfway through the interview I innocently asked her how she liked the class this year. She sighed, audibly. "Oh, they're an OK class," she confided. "A very steady group, but there are no bright lights in the class."

I inquired, almost on impulse: "Precisely how dim is our son on the brightness scale?" She missed the joke, but all that year we saw what happens when we choose a certain set of glasses to see the world. The class performed with predictable dullness and we were glad when the year ended.

As fate would have it, the fourth grade teacher was young and fresh. When I asked her what she thought of the class, she quickly replied, "They're a great group, fun and very smart." Not surprisingly, she and the kids had a very different experience.

I've spent most of my career speaking to people, hundreds of thousands of people, first as a minister speaking to the flock, then as a trainer teaching customer service, and now as an author leading workshops and addressing conferences. Being in front of people and talking has been my whole life, yet as a child I was very shy and kept mostly to myself. Even now, people who meet me at parties or social gatherings have a hard time imagining me standing in front of a large audience giving "motivational" talks. Someone once asked: "What do you do before a speech, go into the phone booth and put on your cape?" I suspect it was not a compliment.

Over the years, many funny moments have happened during my speaking and, along with those lighter vignettes, a few important lessons have been learned about the "glasses we choose to wear." They are offered here as lessons not only for the speaker, but for day-to-day living as well.

The first post in my days as a minister was as assistant pastor of a small-town church in Ohio. In that assignment, all the ministers in town took turns preaching on Sunday morning at the nursing homes. Some of the homes had elderly folk not much older than those who came to our church; others had residents who were less "cognitively correct." At one of the nursing homes they brought people to the Sunday service regardless of their condition. The philosophy seemed to be that it was good to get them out to activities whether they had an inkling of what was being said or not. The senior minister had suggested using children's stories when preaching at the nursing homes. "They will be able to relate to them," he advised, "because they are like children." So I went one day wearing that set of glasses: These old folks are like children, spare them any real meat.

As the room filled, my palms started sweating. Many people in wheelchairs arrived, some of them smiling, perhaps a little too much, others drooling, one kept touching the man next to her and he kept pushing her away saying, "She's touching me." Oh my goodness, I thought, even children's stories may be too much for this group. I began speaking, having simplified my little children's story as much as humanly possible. No sooner had I started talking, when an agitated woman in the first row turned to her tablemate and said in a loud voice: "What the hell is he saying?" Others had surely wondered this before, but never had someone verbalized it. Gathering my courage, I continued.

To my shock, every 30 seconds or so, she would say it again: "What the hell is he saying?" On I went and she kept repeating it. I "dumbed" down the story, making it simpler and simpler till my mouth was spitting out nothing but drivel. I shortened it to the point that what little sense it made in the first place dissipated into the air. When I finished I vowed never to preach there again. A few kind souls told me how well I had done but most sat with blank stares as the attendants wheeled them back to their rooms.

What did I learn from that experience? Well, perhaps my lenses had been the wrong ones. Maybe I had not given them enough credit. I had come thinking they would not be with it enough to hear the real stuff. So I played it safe and told them a children's story and shared little of myself.

In spite of my promise never to return, I did go back, and this time simply shared my story. I told them about my father and how he had died when I was very young and that all my life I have lost people I cared about. They were older than me and surely knew this bitter truth better than I did. It is hard to lose things and to lose people. But each time I lost something, if my heart was open, God gave me new things and new people to love and care about. Why do we have to lose things, I asked rhetorically? I had no answer for them, but God can resurrect our hopes. Sure, a few of the people in the room missed the point of my story, but the ones who did hear me had heard me share my own honest heart—and they responded.

A number of years ago I was to speak to several hundred rural city councilors from the prairies of Canada. I had been on the road for weeks and had little time to prepare. As my talk approached, my wariness grew. What did I know about rural life, having lived in big cities most of my life? What did I know about being a city councilor? After dinner and drinks, why would this group of simple folk want to hear a city boy babble on about the soul of their town? As my time to speak approached, I convinced myself that they were in no mood to hear me or any speaker, that I knew so little about their world that I could not possibly help them and they certainly had not a lick of interest in my topic. Wearing this set of glasses, I spoke for an hour. Predictably, my talk was received with quiet, polite restraint. They sat and endured, I spoke and endured, and after an hour it was mercifully over.

Unlike most of my talks, not one person came up to comment afterward. Just as I was about to leave the conference center in utter discouragement, one man stopped me. "You were the speaker, weren't you?" he asked.

"Yes," I responded, hoping for a compliment about how my talk had moved him.

I was shocked when he turned to his friend and said, "I told you so; he just looks taller up on the stage." My heart sank. I informed my agent not to book me again for an audience so disinterested in my message.

A few weeks later I related my tale of woe to a friend. She said, "Whenever I'm about to speak to a group, I look myself in the mirror and tell myself: 'This is a great group and they want to hear my message!'" I grunted that it was an "interesting technique" and muttered to myself about "motivational speakers."

A few weeks later, history was about to repeat itself. At the end of ten days on the road, my audience was a group of government workers in a department that had been downsized. Those remaining had been working there since they were twenty years old and were staying for the pension (so I had been told). This was their annual meeting, more bad news had been given, and I was their closing speaker on "Awakening the Soul at Work."

I was despondent that this could be happening to me again so soon. What do I know about government work? Sure, I worked for government once, but I got out when I realized it wasn't for me. I'm an entrepreneur, what do I know about people who have worked for the same employer for twenty-five years? Then I suddenly remembered my friend's little pep talk. Looking myself in the mirror, I sarcastically said, "But this is a good group and they want to hear my message!" Several times I repeated that sentence, to no avail—my psyche would not allow the message to sink in. Finally, staring in the mirror, I told myself, "You don't believe that, do you?"

To get to the stage where I was to speak, I had to take a long walk, passing the audience seated politely at tables. As I passed one table, a middle-aged woman reached out and grabbed my arm. "Are you the speaker?" she asked.

"Yes I am," I responded with trepidation.

"Well, I want you to know this is a great group and they are really ready for your message!" I made my way toward the stage, somehow aware that my signals to the universe had been captured by this woman's intuition and she had said exactly what I needed to hear. Suddenly, the audience looked different to me, as if they might be ready for what I had to share. They looked like real people who wanted to come in and have a good day. So I poured my heart out and talked to them about the soul in tough times; how each one of us creates the climate in which we work; how no matter how hard life is, if we follow a few key principles we can ignite the soul for ourselves and for others. The audience watched and listened intently. Afterward, many of them stopped to tell me that my message was precisely what they needed to hear.

So make no mistake: The glasses we choose to wear, the lenses through which we choose to experience the world, the way we see the people who work with us and for us, these are all choices.

So take a chance on being called Pollyanna: See your students as superior, your children as great kids, your husband or wife with the innocent kindness you possessed when you were first dating, your boss as a wonderful person waiting to be set free, and your employees as wanting to do a good job. Dare to see the world through rose-colored glasses and see how many roses begin to appear.

Tomorrow, as serendipity has it, I am to do an all-day workshop on soul to fifty psychiatrists who are acting like children because the hospital where they work has given them an "unfair shake." They are demoralized and angry and some of them are first-class pains in the butt. Or so I am told. But I know differently: They are a great group and are ready to hear my message.

Getting Past Your Expiration Date

"If you are called to sweep streets, but you sweep them the way Beethoven wrote music, you will never have an unhappy day."
—Martin Luther King, Jr.

When I first met Mrs. O'Donnell she was already sixty-four years old and had been teaching for more than forty years. One year away from retirement, even a casual observer could see the youthful enthusiasm she demonstrated in her classroom full of active, noisy fourth-graders. She seemed to have the bright-eyed innocence and wonder of a recent college graduate, even though she had been doing the same thing for four decades.

I have encountered many teachers (and other professionals) who have lost that innocent wonder—often at a much younger age—and meeting her made me ask: Why is it that some people never lose heart? How do we keep the fires of passion burning in our work? Why do some of us stay innocent and joyful long past our predicted expiration date?

In the world of work, we have a word for those who have lost their sense of wonder; we say they are "burned out." When we say we are burned out, it is our way of raising the white flag, surrendering to the loss of whatever wonder once captivated us in our jobs. Burnout is different than stress because it cannot be relieved with a vacation or time off; it is the work itself that we have fallen out of love with. When we have truly fallen out of love with our work, time off doesn't renew our interest. It merely reinforces that the job just isn't fun anymore.

But how do we keep our innocence and avoid becoming burned out? And why is it that some people never lose their innocence about their job or career no matter how long they do it?

A year after meeting Mrs. O'Donnell, I decided to ask her that very question: "I spend a great deal of time working with people, working on how to keep soul in their work, and I am struck by your youthful enthusiasm for your job. I was wondering, what is your secret?"

She laughed and then gave a simple two-word answer: "No idea." Seeing disappointment in my face, she thought more carefully about my question. After some moments of silence, she gave me this answer.

"I think one of the secrets is that every year, throughout my teaching career, I have always had things I was trying to be better at. That is, no year has gone by that I haven't focused on improving in some key area of teaching. This year I'm working on how I can make the children feel more loved. My eyes are always open to new possibilities. Why, just last week, I sat in on the classes of the four newest teachers in our school. These young teachers come with all kinds of new ideas and in each class I picked up at least one thing I'd like to try this year. When you first start your career," she said, "you're always finding new ways of doing things. Then some people get into a rut. I guess I never found the rut!"

Although she never used the specific word, it seemed to me that she was really talking about the concept of craft. Craft is a wonderful idea and not much used in today's society. We are a microwave culture, and *craft* is a word that hints at the need for patience and time. *Craft* comes from a German word for power and strength; to be a craftsperson is to let our inner power come forth into our outer work. A craftsperson is never fully satisfied because the nature of a craft is to move toward perfection—and perfection is an ideal we cannot achieve. Paying attention to our craft is to look at something we have seen a thousand times and to see more possibilities.

Mrs. O'Donnell had been teaching fourth-graders for most of her life but never stopped looking at her job with fresh eyes, the perspective of a craftsperson. Each year she identified ways she wanted to come closer to perfection. Each term she would visit the classrooms of other teachers and bring back ideas. But, most importantly, she never allowed herself to believe she had exhausted all the possibilities, and it was this posture of innocence that sent her out into the world seeking for more.

A Working Renaissance

The journey toward a renaissance in our work must begin with both the belief that more is possible and the choice to engage with our work as craftspeople, as seekers of perfection, striving to use our fullest inner powers.

A friend told me a story about a housekeeper he met at one of the Disney hotels. Passing a room she was cleaning, he discovered her arranging stuffed animals on the bed. As he entered the room, she informed him that when a family left stuffed animals in the room she liked to arrange them doing things. That day she had arranged them in a circle on the bed around a book as if they were reading stories to each other. "When the family comes back, they will be filled with smiles," she said with joy. Tomorrow she was thinking of arranging them around the coffee table playing poker (complete perhaps with a little bottle of whiskey from the minibar). The housekeeper was always looking for new ways to perfect her job and she told my friend: "Something happens to your day when you see your work this way!"

In my own career, I have witnessed the power of craft to renew my innocence about my work. The primary way I make my living is to speak at conventions and corporate events. Since I have given several thousand of these presentations, the potential for burnout and loss of innocence is very high. How many times can one tell the same story and present similar ideas without losing one's sense of wonder? There have been times in my career when the fire has burned less brightly, when my enthusiasm for the work I do has faded.

What I have discovered is that when I pay attention to the craft of my work in a deeper way, my innocence inevitably returns. When I dig more deeply into one area, learning and honing my skill in a particular aspect of work, the soul engages.

For example, a few years ago I became fascinated with storytelling. I started studying great storytellers, learning about the techniques of storytelling, reading books about it, and watching other speakers and the methods they used to tell tales. Most importantly, I experimented with new techniques in telling my own stories. During this time, my work was infused with much of the same innocent wonder that I had when I began my career.

Another time, through the influence of my coach Ron Arden (one of the finest speech coaches in North America), I focused on the use of silence. For many months, I diligently worked on cultivating more and better use of silence in my talks. I would watch how others used silence and practiced a variety of ways to use this in my speeches. Once again, I discovered that the awe and wonder returned. In each case, "speaking" felt like a new job because I was doing it in such a profoundly different way.

When we pay attention to our craft, we are in fact looking at our old job with a fresh set of eyes. In the process of nurturing our craft we begin to see possibilities and our job becomes a "new" job, as we nurture aspects of our inner powers not yet fully developed. It is reminiscent of a scene at the end of one of my favorite mid-life angst movies, *City Slickers*. Billy Crystal's character has been out on a two-week ordeal, driving cattle across a range, having gone on the trip primarily to rediscover his sense of awe and wonder. His job was the main focus of his disillusionment and, when he returns, his wife asks, "So, are you going to quit your job?"

"No," he replies. "I'm just going to do it better."

Rather than changing jobs, we must often change the way we do the job. The power of shifting our perspective is demonstrated by the many people I have met in my coaching work who have gone back to school in their profession, only to report an increase in satisfaction and engagement. The jobs did not change, but they came back with a fresh set of eyes.

And why would we not lose our innocence and enthusiasm when we do our jobs the same way over and over again for many years? The Chinese written word for "boredom" consists of two characters, one for heart and the other for killing. Boredom kills the human heart, for we are craftspeople most of all, explorers who like discovering better ways to do things. Perhaps we burn out because we stop looking for the deeper experience of craft and cease to identify learning possibilities for ourselves.

Setting the Stage for Artistry at Work

Some workplaces have ritualized the renewal of craft in ways that encourage people to rediscover the possibilities in their work. At the

Park Hotel in North Carolina, employees begin every day with a short meeting in which they focus on what is called "The Topic of the Day." At each department's (housekeeping, front desk, banquet services, etc.) morning meeting, managers ask this simple question: What part of our job do we want to do better and more creatively than we did yesterday? Imagine starting every single workday asking what part of our job we want to do better. Imagine letting each day begin with the freeing of the creative spirit to animate what could become routine activities. Every day begins that way at the Park Hotel. After a short time of practicing this ritual, workers reported that their jobs often had the feel of becoming "new" as craft infused their roles.

Any workplace or worker can incorporate this technique. What is your topic of the day (or week, or month, or year)? What aspect of your job are you trying to see with new possibilities? When is the last time you watched how others did their work (especially people younger or more experienced than yourself) and simply noticed what learning might be available? How are you being a student right now in your career? When did you last think about your current job or profession with the eyes of an artist, asking in what areas you want to achieve a deeper perfection?

Some time ago I met a physician who was well past traditional retirement age—the date they tell us we should expire—and was still practicing his craft (and is it not intriguing that some professions are called "practices," intimating we can never reach perfection; we simply engage in more and deeper practice). His younger partners envied him, because even after decades he had the enthusiasm of a fresh graduate. His spirit was infectious and often produced an unintended result: patients wanting to leave his younger colleagues and become one of his patients instead.

One day his young colleagues got up the courage to ask him his secret. Like Mrs. O'Donnell, Dr. Bob did not have a ready answer for them, but he did have a thought.

"You know, even after all these years, I am always trying things that I think might make me a better physician. Just last year I started experimenting with how to make patients feel more cared for when I did rounds at the hospital. I started reading all the literature I could get my hands on and began experimenting with different behaviors as I did my rounds. Out of that inquiry came several specific ways that my practice has changed. I sit now when I enter a patient's room; I always touch the patient on the arm or hand; and before I leave the room I simply say to them: 'Patients tell me they are often intimidated when the doctor visits them and so they don't ask the questions they want an answer to. So before I go, is there anything you want to ask me?'"

He told them that this "practice" of focusing on areas for greater perfection was one that he began in the middle part of his career when he was losing a bit of his edge: "I just began focusing on getting better, one aspect at a time. I never stopped wondering what it meant to be a better doctor!"

Forty years of practicing to be a doctor and his craft was still being honed. The job changed every year because he never ceased to innocently ask how he himself might change to become a better doctor.

So why do some people never burn out? How do a job, a marriage, a profession, and a life continue to become new again, over and over? There probably is no secret formula, but the journey can begin with a single word: craft.

12

Bake a Cake for the Office Troublemaker

A̶lm̶o̶st̶ ev̶er̶y̶ o̶ff̶ice̶ o̶f̶ a̶ny̶ s̶ize̶ h̶a̶s̶ o̶ne̶—an office trouble-maker. That person whom everyone agrees would not be missed if he or she found another place to work. It may be someone who is negative, a gossip, doesn't do a fair share, badmouths everyone, or is simply out of step.

Although there may be exceptions, most of these people did not start out as the "troublemaker." They were hired because somebody thought they would do a good job and there is a good chance they even did so for a while. But somehow, somewhere along the way, a shift occurred. We lost whatever innocent affection we felt toward this person and they lost whatever love they felt for their work.

How do we recapture that innocence?

A friend who is a nurse said there was a woman in her unit whom everyone disliked. She was negative, didn't pull her weight, backstabbed and was, all in all, someone everyone agreed should

Bake a Cake for the Office Troublemaker

leave. Some coworkers had tried to give this woman feedback, to no avail.

For months my friend thought about what she could do to get through to this person. Hard as she tried, she could come up with no cogent strategy. One Saturday morning, she woke up and had an inexplicable desire to bake a cake for the troublemaker. She had no idea why this notion had come to her or what baking a cake might accomplish, but the only thing she had ever heard this woman say she liked was chocolate. So that Saturday morning my friend started her day by baking a chocolate cake. After looking up the woman's address in the phone book, she took the finished cake to her home.

You can imagine the troublemaker's shock when she opened the door.

"What are *you* doing here?" the woman asked incredulously.

"Well," my friend said, "it is kind of hard to explain. I know you like chocolate and I woke up this morning wanting to bake you a cake, so I did." She held the cake out like an offering to an angry god.

The woman smiled ever so slightly and said: "Well, would you like to come in?"

My friend met the woman's husband and began to get a sense of where some of the negativity came from. For the next hour they sat at the kitchen table, ate chocolate cake, and talked. They did not talk about the woman's attitude or her behavior toward colleagues; they simply enjoyed small talk and ate cake.

Monday morning the woman arrived at work, the same grumpy person she had been the week before—but with one notable exception: She was nice to my friend. The next day she even brought my friend a coffee to start the day. Over the next few weeks, they slowly became friendly to the point where they were able to have a heart-to-heart conversation about the workplace. Encouraged by the friendship she felt with my friend, the woman slowly started becoming more positive, began asking others for feedback on how

87

REDISCOVERING THE JOY OF WORK

she could be a better team member. Eventually she regained the innocent enthusiasm she had when she started her job. It took months, but it did happen.

How do we start again with someone who has wronged us at work? What do we do when everything else we have tried has failed to get through to someone? It seems to me that we must begin with kindness, with the courage to reach out with no expectations at all. It begins when we decide to be the one friend to the friendless, the one person reaching out when everyone else has shut down, the one who will care enough to be innocent again.

A friend who is a manager told me about one of his employees who was "hell on wheels." Tempted to read him the riot act one more time, my friend resisted and instead invited him out for coffee. At the table, he said: "You don't seem very happy to me and it's showing in how you act and feel at work. It must be hard to be so unhappy. What is happening for you? I'm wondering if there's anything I can do to help?" The manager spoke the words with such honest sincerity that the man let down the wall which he had so assiduously built and opened up. He began to speak about how he was feeling at this stage of his career: lost, a failure, disliked by others. For the first time they had an honest, frank, open conversation. A miracle did not happen that day, but suddenly it felt as if they were on the same side.

When I was growing up in Staten Island, New York, we lived in a neighborhood filled with immigrants from the Old World: Germans, Italians, Irish, and Poles. Next door to us was a grumpy old Italian man, so mean that he used to threaten us kids with an enormous scythe if an errant baseball found its way into his yard. Nobody was friends with Mr. Morelli and no one got along with him—with one exception.

Across the street from our house lived a kid we knew to be "mentally retarded." His name was Johnny Beatafeld and he was the butt of many jokes. Maybe because he wasn't very smart, or possibly because he was more innocent then the rest of us, he would go over and talk to Mr. Morelli. He didn't know that no one got along with Mr. Morelli. While the rest of us assumed the old man was unreachable, Johnny innocently walked over to the fence and struck up conversations. They became the best of pals. Even as a young person I wondered what might have happened if a few more of us had just as innocently gone to the fence and started talking.

Got a troublemaker in your office? Have a neighbor with whom no one gets along? Have an employee with whom you have tried everything, all to no avail? Well, how about this: bake a cake, walk over and start a chat, let them know that you care, and ask honestly what is happening for them. Let that innocent part of you—the part that is not so jaded as to believe you already know the outcome—go on over and give it a try. Sure, they may not eat the cake, they may not want to chat, but there is something about an innocent act of kindness that even the grumpiest of us can't resist.

And if *you* happen to be the office troublemaker or the neighborhood curmudgeon, remember it is never too late to change your stripes.

13

The Leader's Choice

When I graduated from seminary in 1981, I was twenty-four years old. Within two years, mostly because I was a good preacher, I was hired to be the senior minister at the Brownlee Woods Presbyterian Church in Youngstown, Ohio. At the tender age of twenty-six, the church hired me to be their senior leader.

For the ten years before I arrived, the church had been in a steady decline. Membership was shrinking, attendance declining, revenues at a plateau and, most worrisome of all, the average age of the members was increasingly elderly. Looking out on Sunday morning the blue and gray hairs far outnumbered all others. So the church elders, in their wisdom, hired me in hopes that I would bring in members and gather youth back to the fold.

As this was my first real position of authority, I arrived with the innocent passion and enthusiasm of most young leaders. My innocence took many forms. For one thing, I believed that the people I had been called to lead were capable of doing great things. My faith in them was unlimited and I believed that, given the chance, they would rise to the occasion and work with me to renew the organization, welcoming new members and new ideas with open arms. Like many young leaders, I was also very confident that I knew what it would take to turn things around. Filled with plenty of opinions about what the "older" leaders had done wrong, I was certain I could lead this dying church on the road to renewal. In my youthful enthusiasm, I dreamed great visions of the future and pictured the empty parking lot filled with cars and the church filled with young families.

It was not long into my assignment that reality started to set in. My first realization of how hard it was going to be came when I began making small changes in the Sunday morning worship service. The church was not known to be the friendliest place on the planet. One younger member jokingly warned me that, among the members, "Many are cold and a few are frozen" (a pun on a saying of Jesus: "Many are called but few are chosen"). Undaunted, I decided to begin a time of greeting during the church service where people would walk around and greet each other, especially those who were visitors. Given the old-fashioned views of many members, I felt it prudent to give them a month's warning. One of the newer members could not wait and started doing it that first Sunday, only to be chided by a long-time member: "Oh stop it, sonny, I've got another month before I have to greet you!" This turned out to be a harbinger of things to come.

My first big battle as leader was fought because of a sign. Our church was on a main thoroughfare over which thousands of cars passed every day. Unfortunately, the parking lot faced the street and the church itself was set far back and could hardly be seen from the road. A person could drive by our church a hundred times and not even know it was there. If a driver did notice us, he would not learn the name of the church or anything about us.

In my innocence, I made a suggestion: "What if we put a sign on the street—a large sign—so that no one could pass the church and not know we're here?" I wasn't talking about a big neon sign, but a dignified brick sign, built in a tasteful style with a place where we could put messages for all to see. "Every day," I insisted, "thousands of people will drive by and see our inspirational messages. The sign will be a magnet, drawing people to the fold." What's more, I assured them, we could get such a sign for just $3,000!

It was as if I'd suggested we stage a lynching at the annual church picnic or have the choir sing naked (which definitely would not have attracted new members). The elders were split evenly, with half thinking this was the greatest idea since sliced bread and half thinking their new young leader had lost his mind. The church treasurer accused me publicly of "not giving a hoot about the church's finances!" For months we squabbled about the sign until finally, in a close vote, I won. The sign would be built.

As the months passed, many more battles were fought over everything from changing the church service to providing a divorce recovery workshop for the community. One of the biggest debates we had concerned the use of our education wing. As it sat empty every weekday, I pushed the elders to invite a local preschool to use the facility during the week so that young families would be exposed to our congregation. I won each one of these key decisions—but my enthusiasm, my innocence as a leader, was dying bit by bit.

By the end of two and a half years, I was deeply discouraged. Why could my congregation not see the wisdom of my leadership and, more importantly, the rightness of the direction I was taking the church? What had happened to the enthusiastic young leader who was now disheartened and doubting himself?

When I arrived I had believed in my people, believed they would work with me to achieve our vision. When I arrived I felt I knew the answers. When I arrived I felt our vision would soon be within our reach. Now, two years later, I saw my people as an obstacle; I no longer felt I knew the right answers; my enthusiasm had become discouragement; I was at a loss as to what I should do. I had no idea how to reclaim the hope with which I had begun my assignment. So I did the next best thing—I quit.

Almost twenty years have passed since the day I left that church and many times I wish I could go back and visit that twenty-six-year-old pastor, sit in his office for an hour and tell him what I know now about second innocence in leadership. How I'd jump at the chance to tell my younger self what I have learned!

If it was possible for me to jump into a time machine and go back to visit my younger self, these are the four lessons I would share:

Lesson #1: Never lose your faith in people, but give up your childish hopes
The first thing I would tell that young pastor is that he was right about his people: They really did have it in them to make the church grow and serve the community in a deeper way. But it would take time and he would have to be patient. What's more, I would tell him that the moment he lost faith in his people, the game was over. I expected the congregation to simply rise up and follow and spent very little time nurturing them. They needed a mentor, a coach. What's more, the moment my view of them shifted, my leadership was doomed. The moment I began to see them as an obstacle, the world of possibilities shut down. What they needed was my encouragement and I gave them precious little of that. I began to see them as the "enemy."

Some readers are no doubt thinking that this situation could never happen to them. However, in my eighteen years of consulting I have seen this phenomenon repeated hundreds of times in a variety of situations. A leader starts out with great enthusiasm about his or her people. But people are people and disappoint us in some way. Soon the leader becomes jaded and starts saying things such as: "These union people just don't care. Those old employees have been here so long, we'll never make it until they are gone. If I had not inherited that old leadership team we would be halfway home. People are just plain lazy these days. You just can't find good help anymore. These people will never get with the program." When I was in ministry, this cynicism about people sometimes took the form of a one-liner I had heard scores of other ministers say: "What this church needs is a few good funerals!"

I would suggest that to achieve renewal we must choose to see people with a fresh set of eyes, and to let go of whatever reasons we have written them off. While our initial enthusiasm and faith in people almost always turns out to be naïve, we must realize it is the job of leaders to call forth the hero in each person. We must realize that although people have the ability to be lazy, they also have an innate desire to excel. I have often asked leaders if they think most people wake up in the morning, look themselves in the mirror and say these words before they go to work: "I want to do a poor job today. I want customers and co-workers to regret that I ever took this job. I want to provide poor service and come home at the end of the day bored and frustrated, feeling I have accomplished nothing." Leaders laugh, but I have discovered that it is easy to become jaded about people, to begin to believe that they think those kinds of thoughts.

If I could visit myself at age twenty-six, I would ask, "John, do you think your church members get up in the morning, look in the mirror and say: 'I want to make new people feel unwelcome. I want to stand in the way of all new ideas because I want this church to die a slow death and have my name on the death certificate?" What my people needed was for me to have more faith in them than they even had in themselves, but I let my faith die.

But there is a corollary to this lesson. I would tell myself to give up my childish innocence, the part of me that felt that everyone had to be on board for us to make progress. As I look back now we *were* making real progress, and the vast majority of the people in the church felt I was taking the congregation in the right direction. But, like many inexperienced leaders, I wanted everyone behind me. I needed a more mature view of leadership, one that recognized that you can never win every single person. I needed to focus on those who were leading with me and help them become even stronger. In time, others would either have joined the parade or dropped out. I had to learn that leaders are not always liked by everyone, that this is a naïve, childish wish that has little to do with the real world of leadership. What's more, by focusing on those who were not aligned, I became discouraged and gave up. I needed to keep my faith in people and lose my need for them to like me.

Lesson #2: You don't have to have all the answers

The second thing I would say to my younger self is: A leader does not need to have every answer. Be open and listen to others.

One of the things I have discovered in my work with organizations is that many leaders suffer from a terminal case of "knowing." We feel that being a leader means we are supposed to have all the answers. So we pretend to be the ones who know, and thus shut out the need for others to search for answers. Our people depend on us to give answers—and they blame us when they are not the right ones.

As a young leader, I believed I knew the answers, but—more importantly—I felt my congregation needed me to know the answers. Knowing what I know now, I would tell myself to ask more questions, to get my people asking the right questions such as: What do we need to do to renew this church? What do we each need to do to make it vibrant and vital again? How will we have to change to get the results we want?

People do want us to have some answers, but maturity in leadership is about knowing that the answers must ultimately come from within each one of us. Maturity in leadership is knowing that even if we did have all the answers, they would only be *our* answers. Leadership is about helping people come to their own conclusions. It takes time for a leader to realize this. It takes time to be able to say: "I don't know."

What's more, I needed to grow at least as much or more than my congregation. I would tell my younger self to find a few good mentors, to find leaders with more experience who had accomplished the renewal I was seeking. I might even tell my younger self to be like a child, to ask lots of questions, to know that he does not know. I think far too many leaders let their egos get in the way of their learning. When we are young we think we know it all, so we don't seek mentors. When they do come along, we are too busy trying to show them what we already know—so they often move on to those who are more open. By the time we admit we need mentoring, we are at an age where people are coming to us to be a mentor!

I would plead with my younger self to find a good mentor and to learn all I could. To be as innocent as a young child, asking every question I could think to ask. One is never too old to be a novice, to admit that you do not know. When we have the courage to admit that, mentors will arrive to guide us.

Lesson #3: Focus on the why—and the how will follow

If I could spend that hour with my twenty-six-year-old self, this is what I would want to say most of all: "John, it was not about the sign!" I really believed we were fighting over the sign and I could not, for the life of me, understand why the elders in my church would argue so vehemently over building a $3,000 brick sign. How petty could they be? And because I believed we were fighting over the sign, I missed the real issue. Twenty years later I know we were really fighting over our identity as a congregation. Instead of talking about the sign, we should have been having hours of conversation about what kind of a congregation we wanted to be.

Did we want to be *in* the community or *outside* of it? If we wanted to grow, how would our own self-image have to change or evolve? What was the place risk would play in our renewal? And why did we exist at all—what was our real mission? But these were not the conversations we had. Instead we fought about the sign, changes in the worship service, the addition of staff, and a day care center moving into the church basement.

This reminds me of the motorcycle manufacturer Harley-Davidson, one of the great turnaround stories of modern business. On the brink of bankruptcy, the leaders at Harley pursued a radical course of action: They began to involve front-line people in all significant decisions. The company's success story is well known. Today, the company readily admits that it takes a longer time to reach decisions at Harley than at the competition. But Harley-Davidson also says that when it implements an idea it does so much faster than competitors. The company has worked incessantly on the why and avoids most of the fights about "signs."

Lesson #4: Discouragement is part of the leadership game
There is one final word of wisdom I would offer that young minister, sitting discouraged in his office, on the brink of quitting. I would tell him that discouragement is an integral and important part of any leader's evolution. I would tell him that every leader—from Martin Luther King, Jr. and Mohandas Gandhi to most of the great statesmen of business—had moments when they felt they were accomplishing little, when their innocent faith in themselves and in others was deeply wounded. These periods of discouragement can be the portal to renewal if they are approached with an open heart. Who knows what I might have learned had I stayed past that low point of discouragement? Ironically, I left at the very moment my heart might have been most open to learning.

What Does It Mean to Be Innocent as a Leader?

So what does it mean to be innocent as a leader? It means to not allow our view of those we lead to become jaded, to continue to see the potential in others for greatness even when they let us down—which they inevitably will in some way.

It means to know that we do not know, to be open to the answers others may provide. It is to be a childlike leader who asks lots of questions about why and how, knowing that there is a world of answers waiting for those who have lots of questions.

It means to be willing to be a novice again and again, to continue to be a learner—not merely the one who teaches. It is continually to seek mentors at whatever level we have reached and never stop finding things at which we want to be better.

It means to accept that discouragement is part of the game and can be the very portal to deeper insight.

The End of the Story

Just last year, I was driving from Cleveland to Pittsburgh and passed through Youngstown and could not resist visiting my old church. As I drove into the parking lot, the first thing I noticed was the sign, still there and looking pretty good almost two decades later. Although there was no one in the church, the doors were open, so I walked in.

As I entered the foyer, the emotions of twenty years ago entered me with a surprising immediacy. I could recall the enthusiasm and hope that filled me when I preached there for the first time. I could remember looking out at the people and dreaming great things. But I could also feel in my gut the sense of failure that burdened me the day I left, how discouraged I was and how I laid the blame for those failures at the feet of my parishioners.

In the foyer were pictures of members at recent activities and to my surprise there were people I still recognized (though—like me—they had quite a few more wrinkles). The pictures were worth a thousand words: The congregation had continued to age, the young families had not returned in large numbers. The opportunity for renewal had occurred on my watch, but I had not been ready.

Sitting in the front pew, I wondered how many leaders might be losing their innocence that very day, ready to lose faith in their people and themselves, moving towards cynicism.

Maybe I had to lose my innocence. Maybe the path to wisdom always runs through the valley of mistakes and discouragement.

And maybe it is not until we lose our way that we realize how much innocence is at the core of what it takes to lead.

PART III

Rediscovering Innocence in Relationships

Perhaps nowhere in our lives is the
rediscovery of innocence as challenging or as
important as in the realm of relationships. And this may
be because—of all the areas of our lives—rediscovering joy in
this realm requires the participation of other human beings: our
partners, our children, our families, and our friends.

It has always seemed to me that other than food and basic security, there are only two fundamental human drives: the drive to achieve and the drive to connect with others. Indeed in casual conversations with people, it is evident what a central place family and friends play in our lives.

Having said that, it is also clear that relationships are tough and difficult to sustain. The divorce rate in the developed world is but one reminder of how hard it is to keep the wonder and joy in relationships. In fact, there may be more cynical jokes about marriage than perhaps any other human institution. Hence, Jean Paul Sartre said in his play *No Exit:* "Hell is other people." And, one could add, so is heaven.

This section explores how we can cultivate more joy
and innocence in our relationships.

14

Finding Perfect Love

In Western society, we believe one of life's primary goals is finding the perfect mate. This helps explain why so many single people spend so much time looking for Mr. or Ms. Right. We have been told through movies and fairy tales to search for the perfect love— the one person with whom we will simply live "happily ever after."

I have one love that will always remain perfect and completely innocent.

Lynn and I met after my second year in college when I left New York City to spend four months working at an inner-city community center in Chicago. At the time, the decision to go there was a big one for me, having been very shy in high school and plagued with severe acne. Flying across the country to a place where I knew no one was a big risk, one that would forever change my life.

I remember vividly the day I arrived in Chicago when Nancy Ames, director of Jones Community Center, picked me up at O'Hare Airport. It was a hot, sunny day in early June and we rode in her old convertible, top down, along the shores of Lake Michigan heading south. It was the first time I had been more than five hours from home, my first time on an airplane, the first time truly away from my family—and my first real choice to risk failure. With the wind blowing in my hair, my heart was filled with an intense mix of absolute terror and exhilaration.

As the summer progressed, some of us who worked at the center wound up being cast in the summer production of the musical *Kiss Me, Kate* at Prairie State College. As a college kid from New York, complete with Rocky Balboa accent, I was typecast perfectly as the lead gangster in the Cole Porter classic.

In the chorus of the show was a young, bubbly, twenty-year-old named Lynn, just back from her sophomore year at Bradley University. As I mentioned in Chapter 4, I never took much notice of Lynn until a friend of mine, partly to get me to stop bugging his sister Kay for a date, told me that Lynn was interested in me. He offered to arrange a double date and he did. I can still remember our first kiss, standing late at night by the white picket fence outside her family's farmhouse in Crete, Illinois. After the kiss, I nervously asked the big question: "So . . . would you like to see me again?"

With no hesitation and a wide smile on her face, she said, "Of course, silly," before she ran into the house.

Lynn was everything I could have wanted in a woman: thoughtful, sensitive, fun, outgoing, a person of faith, smart and attractive. She was also very interested in the "kid from New York who was planning to become a minister." Over the next several weeks we had a series of dates and got to know each other as part of the daily four-hour rehearsals for the show. My excitement at getting to know her was growing, my sense of myself as a human being deepening. July 4th was approaching and her large family was having a big picnic. Lynn invited me to join them.

The day before the picnic, the costumes for the show arrived at O'Hare Airport. My friends John and Wally were going in a van to pick them up and asked Lynn and me if we wanted to join them. We both said that we didn't care, but if the other wanted to go we were game. As I think back on it now, I think neither of us wanted to go all that much, but we did want to spend more time together that day and needed an excuse. I remember I was wearing the most awful red, white, and blue shorts (this was the unfashionable '70s) and sat on the floor of the open cargo section of the van as we rode to the airport, Lynn's arm resting on my thigh. And I remember her smile. In that moment, forever frozen in my mind, life was perfect.

When we arrived at the cargo area at O'Hare, John went to check on the costumes. We were parked next to an airport runway and could see the planes taking off. Lynn said: "I'd love to get a better look at those planes. Somebody boost me up so I can get on top of the van!" Wally obliged, putting his hands together to help her up. As she tried to get hold of the top of the van she started to slip, Wally got spooked, let go of her feet and Lynn fell backward. Her feet hit the edge of the open cargo door and she fell backward, her head hitting the concrete road with the full force of a six-foot freefall.

Jumping out of the van I ran over to Lynn. She was incoherent, her feet moving back and forth. I put my hand under her head and yelled for an ambulance. For the next few moments, while Wally ran to get help, there were just the two of us by the van, her head cradled in my hand. Gently rubbing her hair, I kept saying: "It will be OK, Lynn, it will be OK."

As she lay there, I brushed her hair away so I could see the back of her scalp; there was no blood. But what I saw was a symmetrical ring of red dots on her scalp, almost like someone had drawn it on her head. In spite of having no medical training a thought ran through my mind: "She's bleeding inside." I was right.

Riding in the ambulance beside the driver, I heard the paramedic utter words I will never forget: "She's stopped breathing!"

They put her on a respirator and when she arrived at Resurrection Hospital in suburban Chicago, doctors operated for five hours.

While she was in surgery, I remember sitting in the tiny hospital chapel, tears running down my face, consumed by a grief I had never felt before. Being a young man of faith, planning to enter the ministry, I pleaded with God for her life.

Lynn never regained consciousness. For twenty-four days, including the opening night of *Kiss Me, Kate*, she remained comatose in that bed at Resurrection Hospital until one day when she simply expired. Her last words had been spoken to me as she lay on that concrete parking lot and I was unable to understand them.

Twenty-six years later, she remains frozen in time, forever a twenty-year-old woman, full of life and a new love full of immense possibilities never to be fulfilled. To this day, I wonder what might have happened if we had simply not gone to the airport to pick up the costumes.

For some time after that event, no woman could live up to Lynn. We were together just a short time and our love ended abruptly in the midst of our innocence. I had not yet realized—nor had she—that neither of us was perfect, that we would inevitably disappoint each other in some significant ways, and that we would not live happily ever after.

Lynn will forever be twenty years old, standing by that white picket fence, kissing me good night.

Love and the End of Perfection

To put it in dramatic terms, most intimate relationships begin the way my relationship with Lynn ended. We meet someone and for a number of intoxicating weeks or months (and, in a few lucky situations, years), we believe that this person is our only soul mate. In what some psychologists call the "collapsing of ego boundaries," we believe this person is just like us and will make us whole.

Such innocence almost always dies. One morning we wake up and see another human being, filled with different aims and desires. They are not perfect and, what's more, they realize that we are not perfect either.

As Scott Peck puts it succinctly in *The Road Less Traveled*:

> Just as reality intrudes upon the two-year-old's fantasy of omnipotence, so does reality intrude upon the fantastic unity of the couple who have fallen in love. Sooner or later, in response to the problems of daily living, individual will reasserts itself. He wants to have sex; she doesn't. She wants to go to the movies; he doesn't. He wants to put money in the bank; she wants a dishwasher. She wants to talk about her job; he wants to talk about his. She doesn't like his friends; he doesn't like hers. So both of them, in the privacy of their own hearts, begin to come to the sickening realization that they are not one with the beloved, that the beloved has and will continue to have his or her own desires, tastes, prejudices and timing different from the other's.[3]

Second Innocence in Intimacy

Experiencing a second innocence in intimacy may be the toughest journey of all the mysterious realms explored in this book. Tougher than experiencing renewal in faith, more elusive than the reanimation of daily life, and far less linear than a reawakening at work, it is something many people never know. Unlike renewal in daily life, work, and faith, the reanimation of love requires the participation of another human being.

The reasons for its elusiveness have many roots, not the least of which is the intense intoxication we often feel during the first stages of love. Most of us have experienced the rush of new love, along with its power to overwhelm us. It comes upon us, like the answer to all our prayers, in the form of an erotic storm of sensual and emotional energy.

This first stage in intimacy is almost always about us. If we are honest, our first attraction to someone is not usually about what we can do for them, but about what they can do for us. Will she arouse my sexual interest? Will she look good on my arm? Will he raise my social status and provide me comfort? Will I enjoy his company? Will our values match? Can we build a lifestyle that suits my needs or fantasies? Even for those who find themselves attracted to partners who "need them," such an attraction is often based more on one's own need to take care of someone than it is about that other person's wish to be cared for.

During this first innocence I may care about this other person, but I am attracted to what I perceive she may do for me. This is precisely why so many people leave relationships when they no longer feel their needs are being met.

For example, my wife Leslie and I met when she was a student in one of my corporate workshops. When she walked into the room her beauty and vitality captivated me. She was a lovely, youthful, twenty-eight-year-old with the most piercing blue eyes. During the workshop she was the consummate rebel, challenging each of my points. Both of us remember those first few hours together, how we could not take our eyes off each other, the intense attraction we felt even though we had only a casual conversation in the hall during a break. For the next two months I could not get her off my mind.

We started dating six months later; it was both intense and electrifying. Certain that she was the "one," I marched headlong into a fiery long-distance relationship. Within a month, the words "I love you" had been spoken and the future pledged. There were moments of great pleasure, close companionship, wonderful laughter, vehement arguments, and intense sexual pleasure. And I do believe we were in love.

But this stage did not last. It never does. Slowly, over time, the ego boundaries were rebuilt. Many people feel this headlong "fall" into romance is the very essence of love and they find themselves deeply disappointed when this stage ends. Having experienced this fall from grace, they spend the rest of their lives trying to recreate that first rush of emotions that characterized the early moments of intimacy.

At the other extreme are those who suggest love is not an emotion at all, but rather a commitment to care for another human being. This line of reasoning suggests that romantic love is always fleeting, ultimately frivolous, and that long-term intimate relationships are based primarily on friendship and commitment rather than passionate emotion. If we want to experience a renaissance in a relationship, we must let go of these romantic notions and focus on developing a deep, enduring friendship. This is compelling, but it ignores a basic fact: Emotion and sexuality are at the heart of intimate human relationships. The idea that we must give up these elements of early love in order to experience a deeper innocence seems too easy a resolution to the dilemma of long-term intimacy.

Somehow then, second innocence in intimacy must incorporate the eroticism and emotions of early romance while moving toward a deeper connection based on spiritual growth.

Many couples get married in the midst of their first innocence and spend a lifetime trying to make that other person live up to fantasy. Others never commit, choosing instead to go from one love to the next, exiting before the hard work begins—like Peter Pan. This choice means loving only as a child loves. Such a love is based on what the other person gives me, missing all the deeper complexities of a love based on spiritual growth, the only truly compelling reason for two humans to spend a life together.

Others lose their passion, waking up one morning to discover they don't love their mate anymore, at least not as they did before. Confronted with this loss of erotic electricity, their relationship settles into a deep friendship at best, a tense arrangement of convenience at worst. It is my belief that neither friendship nor unions of convenience represent second innocence in intimacy.

Second innocence should not be confused with "settling." There are people who convince themselves that true love is simply about companionship. For the sake of the kids, the life savings, the expediency of it all, or to be practical, they may choose to have what used to be termed a marriage of convenience. True affection and spiritual regard are replaced by a conscious choice to tolerate this other person. After all, they tell themselves, there is no perfect love!

Rather than settling for something less, evolution in intimacy is about embracing something deeper. Unlike the first innocence in love in which we are blind to the faults of our lover, in second innocence we see beyond his or her faults to the human being beneath the imperfections. We recognize our lover not as a soul mate (that is, the one who fulfills us), but as the wholly other spiritual being he or she is, replete with his or her own desires and will, and in whose presence completion may be found only within oneself.

This may explain why most studies of long-term happy marriages suggest that these unions become more like long-term friendships than what we normally think of as "romantic lovers." That is not to say that such couples do not have orgasmic lovemaking, that they do not experience moments of sheer ecstasy from time to time, but that the relationship has the characteristics of a mature friendship: unconditional love, complete regard for this person's well-being, acceptance of their wonderful "otherness," and a focus not on what this person can do for "me," but how I can be of assistance to them.

Falling in Love vs. Stepping into Love

When we first meet someone, we often speak of "falling" in love with him or her. Yet second innocence in love is perhaps more a "stepping" in love. Falling is something beyond our control, the strike of Cupid's arrow, but stepping is an act of will, the choice to embrace this person for all that he or she is and may yet become.

Falling in love the second time we realize that we are responsible for our own happiness and that we love as a path to spiritual growth as well as a path to selfish ecstasy. But how do we move toward a deeper intimacy with another person?

We move toward deeper levels in love when we are willing to live in this tension between desire and commitment. It is a choice to love regardless, to love the person for who he or she is, to seek the lover's ultimate spiritual happiness even if the pursuit of that happiness conflicts with our own. It is a commitment to continually renew the flame of desire, to bring the sensual pleasure that is central to our humanity back into our relationships instead of away from it and to do the hard work necessary to renew that primal energy. It is to accept that if we choose to be in a long-term relationship with another person, the initial rush of collapsed ego boundaries must end and make way for something deeper. And it is ultimately to choose not to settle for an arrangement, a union of convenience that robs us of the deep intimacy of which all the poets have written.

The Living, Loving Process

Like all elements of our lives, love is a daily experience, a living process that unfolds in small moments, not in momentous events. One of the ways we cultivate this loving process is by recognizing the ebb and flow of intimacy—that there are moments when love is near and moments when it is far from us, even in the best of relationships. When we are reminded again why we love this person, it is cause for deep celebration. It is also recognizing that these moments, naturally, come and go. To expect each day to mimic the first time together is not realistic, but if we are awake, these moments of wonder come often enough to rekindle that initial fire.

Recently, just before bedtime, I was telling my wife about a book I was reading and what the characters were experiencing, reflecting on the meaning of that experience for our lives. Her eyes lit up, she reached out and gently grabbed my chin, kissing me softly on the lips. "That is the man I love," she said. It was one of those moments when I had done something small, which served as a reminder of what she first loved in me—the intellectual, the thinker, the brooder on the meaning of things. For a brief moment she returned to the beginning of our relationship and experienced a renaissance of affection. Love is like this; it is not blissful moment after blissful moment.

There are ways to be deliberate in rediscovering the beloved. It is not necessary to leave this to chance. At one of our retreats, a woman told me that she had been married for twenty years and happily so. When she and her husband were on their honeymoon they started a small discipline. Each night before bedtime they would tell each other one thing the other person had done that day which reminded them of why they fell in love in the first place. "On the honeymoon," she said, "it was really easy. There were so many little things each day."

When they returned from their honeymoon they continued the ritual. Every night before they went to sleep they would tell each other one thing the other had done that day that reminded them of why they had decided to spend their lives together. She admitted that after twenty years, there were some nights about two hours before bedtime when she would ask herself, "What in the world am I going to say?" On a particular day, her husband may have done scores of things that made her wish she had never laid eyes on him. "But," she concluded, "we have had a profoundly soulful marriage because for twenty years we have ended every day being attentive to the moments that ignite our intimacy." Many people who have heard me speak have tried this simple technique and reported good results in restarting the affection in their relationship. One couple began during their engagement with great impact. Such disciplines are a way of returning to innocence.

Sometimes the breakthrough moments come when the life cycle offers us a fresh chance to rediscover one another. For example, when the children leave home and the nest becomes empty, couples are often given a unique opportunity to rediscover their romance— or to let it go. Extramarital temptations, life changes of various kinds—these are all moments in which we may need to commit to the nurturing of love. In a healthy, long-term partnership we may get "divorced" numerous times. The relationship we have at any given time in its life cycle may have to die to make way for a new marriage born at this stage of personal evolution. We cannot pretend that we have one marriage for forty years; such a situation could only be possible if two people remained stagnant for this entire length of time, which would be a form of dying. Our relationships are ever in flux and continually offer the opportunity for deeper intimacy.

One of the ways we reanimate relationships is to be more deliberate in cultivating both romantic love and spiritual companionship. When we first enter a relationship, part of the innocence we experience is an artifact of novelty. This new person is like a beautiful piece of fruit and we peel away the outer layer to see what's beneath. After a time we may conclude that we know all there is to know about this person . . . and other fruit begins to tempt us. But, if we are honest, we realize we stopped peeling!

When we are first together we put all kinds of time and energy into getting to know this person, discussing what we believe and how we see the world. We dress to impress and try hard to know what they are interested in. We make an all-out effort to nurture love and a spiritual connection.

Intimate relationships may suffer from the same lack of attention to craft that diminishes our love for work. When we first enter a relationship we are deeply attentive to the "art" of love, thinking carefully about how each aspect of our craft might woo and win our lover. Within each realm of the relationship—the gifts we give, the dates we plan, even the lovemaking we perform—we approach love with the mind of the artisan seeking perfection. But, after a time, all these areas become routine: The gift becomes a last-minute purchase at the mall just before the special day; the lovemaking is done as it has been for years with little thought to artistry, let alone variety; the dates we have are not planned with imaginative flair, but with endless predictability ("Want to go to a movie tonight?").

This lack of attentiveness can be seen in the topics we choose to talk about with our partners. When my wife and I were first together, we spent hours on the phone discussing life, people, politics and so forth. After several years of marriage we spent most of our time talking about the finances, who was picking up the kids, what car we were going to buy. . . .

At a recent banquet, I was at a table filled with strangers. The conversation was free-flowing and vibrant, with topics ranging across wine, politics, foreign travel, romance, business. Later someone observed that at home we speak rarely about these things with those we love most. Perhaps we should have nights in our homes when the following subjects are *Off Limits*: the kids, money, chores, and in-laws. There may be silence for a time, but romance and spiritual connection may feel that they have been invited back into the house.

The Science of Intimacy

Aphrodite, the Greek goddess of love and beauty, made a science of knowing what elements stimulated love and attraction. Any man or woman who wants to keep romance in a relationship must follow the path of Aphrodite. Taking time to understand our partner, to become aware of that which ignites the partner's love instincts, is the science of intimacy. We choose to ignore this at our peril.

Too often we behave as if the first romantic months of our relationships are meant to be a meal whose calories will sustain us for decades. Rather, the first stage of a relationship is just an appetizer for the banquet yet to come. As the *Tao* says: "Passion is but a prelude to years of gradual unfolding."[4]

This gradual unfolding is very subtle. Only through years of slow movement do we achieve the deepest levels of love. The choice not to enter into this realm is legitimate, but we must recognize it as a choice. My own instinct and experience tell me that if erotic attraction and spiritual regard were there in large measure when a relationship began, they will return again and again if we pay attention to their nurturance.

Perhaps we might begin with a few simple questions: What would rekindle romance in our relationship? What aphrodisiacs affect my partner? What parts of myself am I willing to reveal as part of the gradual unfolding of our intimacy? How can I move toward selfless love for this person?

On the journey from innocence through disillusionment to a new embrace, there may be moments of betrayal. Extramarital activity—one of those betrayals—is supposedly rampant in Western society. As many as 50 to 60 percent of those responding to surveys admit to being sexually unfaithful during the course of marriage. What are we to make of this as we think about the possibilities of long-term intimacy?

Perhaps we must take it first as a sign, an indicator of the state of our relationship. At a deeper level, it also indicates how much easier it is to experience initial connection than it is to nurture deeper intimacy. But how might our primary relationship be different if we brought the same energy expended in extramarital activity to our committed relationship? How we act differently in these "affairs" may be more significant than how our partners differ from those to whom we are attracted.

Still, the main point is this: It is possible to rekindle intimacy again and again so that, when love deepens, it gradually unfolds to the experience of second innocence, an experience of great worth. And that is worthy of our attempts to create it.

Perfect Love or Enduring Intimacy?

So I have one perfect love, one truly innocent love that can never be stained. But the beautiful memory of it, frozen in time, cannot compare to the connection I share with my wife. Here is what I have learned about love in the twenty-six years since the day of that accident by the side of a van: I would gladly trade my perfect memory of Lynn for the chance to disappoint her. In a heartbeat, I would give up that purity for the opportunity to know her more deeply. Surely our innocence would have ended, but the loss of that would have been worth the chance of what might have come after that loss—the possibility of genuine love.

Genuine love is not love that never disappoints us, but love that always stretches us and challenges us to become a better human being. In this sense, my wife and I have the perfect love. She is wholly other (and sometimes the kind of wholly other that drives me nuts), but I love her unconditionally, have a growing regard for her well-being, am willing to respect who she truly is—as opposed to wishing she were different—and am increasingly focused not on what I can get from her but what I can give to her. We never cease to challenge one another to grow spiritually and emotionally. It is not always pleasant. At the same time, we have chosen through consistent effort and willing spirits to rediscover the fire we both felt that first day in class when our eyes met for the first time. This, I think, is the second innocence.

Yes, you ask, but what is the secret? What mantra can I chant before bedtime to keep the fire burning brightly? Alas, I have no answer. It is a path we must all discover for ourselves. It is a path of spiritual discipline and of loving intention.

I do know that the recipe for renewal in love always contains these ingredients: attention to romance, a willingness to focus on what we can give to another as opposed to what we will get, a respect for the natural cycles of intimacy, a willingness to work hard at keeping a significant spiritual connection with the other person and the patience to let each of these elements evolve.

When my wife and I married it was not the first time either of us had fallen in love. Illusions about every moment being "happy ever after" and love filling every hole we had inside of ourselves had long ago been given up. For our ceremony I wrote a poem for her that expressed some of what I have tried to share in this chapter:

> *Falling in love for the first time*
> *is something you never forget.*
> *When the rush of all desires fills you*
> *convincing you that everything you ever wanted is in your grasp*

> *Falling in love for the last time*
> *is something you never regret.*
> *When something deep inside lays its claim*
> *showing you that everything you ever needed*
> *was inside you.*

> *Falling in love for the last time is like*
> *sweet gentle rain on dry hard land.*
> *The sound and glow of a warm raging fire*
> *on a crisp cold night.*
> *The first taste of cool water*
> *on hot parched lips.*
> *The faint glimpse of land on a journey*
> *that you thought would never end.*

Falling in love for the first time
every naïve wish tells you
it will be easy from this point on.
Falling in love for the last time you see
that it will never be easy again,
Just as it should be,
if you ever want to be more than you were alone.

When I fell in love with you, it was,
now I know,
the first time.

15

The Power of Not Now: Love and the Art of Presence

My son brought home a raffle ticket from school. On the back was clearly printed these words in bold type: *Must Be Present to Win!* It occurred to me as I looked at it that this is precisely true of the journey to intimacy: We must be present to experience the depths that love has to offer—in friendship, in parenting, and in marriage.

As I think about my experiences as a parent, what strikes me is how present most young children are when they are with another person. It is rare to catch a young child looking at the clock while with you. It is this "in the moment" presence that we find most attractive in children. As adults we often speak wistfully of those days when we had the freedom of a child, a time when—because we had no deep concerns—we could be fully present in the now. Somehow as we get older we focus far too much outside of whatever moment we are in.

The ability to recapture the art of being present has much to do with a renaissance in the quality of our relationships. When we are fully present, we communicate deep empathy for others. When we are fully present, five minutes with our children can be "quality time" and, when we are not present, even several hours with loved ones fails to produce the desired effect. Ten minutes of being deeply listened to by a friend is worth several hours with someone whose mind is elsewhere.

The poetic and spiritual traditions are full of references to the power of being in the present moment. In *Walden,* Thoreau wrote about "improving the nick of time." In the Zen tradition there is a saying: "When you sit, sit. When you stand, stand. Don't wobble." That is, stay present, be fully in whatever activity you are in, and know that whenever part of us is somewhere else, the soul cannot fully engage.

Research in the medical field has demonstrated the power of being fully present. In several studies, the behavior of physicians was observed and coded during routine office visits. Researchers observed those physicians who displayed signals of distraction (e.g., multi-tasking, lack of eye contact, hands on the door while asking questions) and those who displayed "mindful" behaviors (e.g., eye contact, one-pointed focus, leaning inward). When patients left the examining room they were asked to guess how much time their doctor had spent with them. On average, patients whose doctors had appeared distracted thought their physicians had spent only half the amount of time they had actually spent interacting, whereas patients of those doctors who appeared to be present reported that they had spent two to three times more time with the doctor than they actually had. Such studies demonstrate the power of presence to impact relationships. In a time when we are all so busy, learning to be mindful can have a significant positive impact on our relationships with spouses, children, friends and co-workers.

I cannot help but think of the number of times my wife and I have been in a conversation and she will stop right in mid-sentence as she is sharing something important with me. She will look at me and say with a hurt voice, "You're not listening to me." Intuitively, in knee-jerk defense, I am inevitably able to parrot back to her the exact last two sentences she has spoken, but inside I am aware of being busted. Although my ears did in fact take the words in and register them in my brain, she was right in her perception—my mind was elsewhere. Cultivating an ability to truly be present with others is central to truly rewarding relationships.

When we think of people who have the gift of creating engaging personal relationships we often describe them as having charisma, meaning they have the unusual ability to arouse devotion in others. As an example, I have known several people who met the late Mother Teresa, and each of them commented on how charismatic she was. Yet, outwardly she demonstrated few of the qualities we normally associate with charisma: She was not a great speaker, was not very gregarious nor did she glad-hand or dress for success. Some time ago I heard an interview with a Catholic priest who spent a year working in the Calcutta mission of Mother Teresa during the last year of her life. In the interview, he was asked about her charisma. He commented that the "amazing thing about her was that when you were in her presence, you felt like you were the most important person in the world. She was fully focused on you and, although she said very little, she was so undistracted that her personal power engaged you." The source of her charisma was her capacity for presence. Many people have said the same of the Dalai Lama.

But how do we stay in the now? How do we learn to be present in the moment-to-moment experience of living and relating in the way we could as children? How do we cultivate an ability to be with others? How do we retrain our minds to become more present and less distracted?

The Present Is When Things Happen

A helpful place to begin is the recognition that we are powerful only in the present moment. Except for thinking about the future or past, the only real power we have to *do* anything is in the present. The past is, for the most part, behind us and we cannot alter it. The future is, by definition, ahead of us. Although we can act in the present moment to influence the future, although we can act in the present moment based on what we have learned from the past, we are in the end always acting only in the present moment. To have our mind focused on the past or the future has only one power over us: It robs us and it robs others of our full attention.

Here are some real examples of the way a focus on the future or the past can rob relationships of joy. Let's say I am at home spending quality time with one of my children and my mind wanders to an incident that happened at work last week. For those moments, the joy available to me in that moment with my child is diverted to an event over which I now have no power. Instead of enjoying my time with my child, my energies are diverted to an event about which I can now do nothing.

My wife wants to speak to me about something important to her. If I am able to give her my one-pointed attention, she will feel my empathy and our relationship will be deepened. If, on the other hand, I allow my mind to wander, she will sense my distraction and our relationship will be diminished. In that moment, if I am present, I will be powerful with the ability to provide love to my wife, but if I am distracted my power is diminished both because I cannot do anything about my distraction and because my wife will not get my full attention.

What's more, the long-term quality of our relationships is diminished by distraction. Over time, those we love can become acclimated to our lack of presence so that they no longer feel empathy even when we are trying to communicate it. A mother told me that her seventeen-year-old daughter became so used to her distrac-tion that when she would ask her daughter about her day, her daughter would start talking and then in the middle of her thought say something like: "And after he beat me up, he ripped off my clothes!" Those words became code for "I know you are not with me." Many times, the mother admitted, "I don't even catch that she says those words—which only reinforces my lack of presence."

Yet, and here is the key point, we can retrain our minds to be more present. The first tool for retraining ourselves is to simply be aware when we become distracted, to notice when our mind wan-ders from the moment we are in. In that moment of awareness, it is critical that we recognize that we, and only we, have the choice about what to do about that distraction.

When the distraction comes, we can ask ourselves a few important questions. The first question might be: Is this thought about the future or past important in terms of influencing the pres-ent moment? That is, is this a distraction or something that should influence how I live this present moment, with the potential to make it more meaningful or enjoyable?

For example, I might be with my wife, about to take a walk in the woods. As we begin our walk, I find my mind thinking about all the work I have to do. I realize that the work has nothing to do with this moment but is only a distraction. In other words, thinking about work at this moment has no potential to enhance the present experience. It is therefore a distraction. If I can clear my mind of this distraction, my wife will get the pleasure of my company.

On the other hand, I might find myself thinking about the walk we took last week. In the middle of that walk, I brought up an issue about work, and my bringing it up ruined the romantic walk for my wife. This thought is not a distraction; it has the power, in this present moment, to influence how I choose to take my walk.

This leads to a second question: Is there anything I want to, can, or need to do about this thought in the present moment? In other words, do I have any power over it right now? In the example above, thinking about all the work I have to do is not helpful because I *cannot* do my work at that moment. I can only ruin my walk. On the other hand, thinking about last week's walk may influence me to choose in the present moment to commit to not mentioning work on this walk. In either case, once these decisions are made (is this a distraction or an important signal, and do I want to do anything about this thought in the present moment), then I still have one final important choice to make: *Do I want to brush aside the thought and stay in the moment or do I want to be distracted?* And make no mistake, the latter is a choice to stay distracted.

A Simple Technique for Becoming Present

We can train our minds to be more present and awake by making choices about what we do with distractions. Meditation is great practice for mindfulness in relationships. When I first learned to meditate, my guide was Debra Klein. Debra led me through a series of techniques for "mindful" meditation that included posture, relaxation, breathing, and focusing exercises. Soon, however, distractions arose. As I meditated, thoughts would race through my head: work, the bills, kids, responsibilities, worries, and so on.

As I struggled with these distractions, I asked Debra what to do about them. She counseled that if I tried to fight with the distractions, they would fight back. Rather, she suggested, you must be gentle with the distractions. When they arise, imagine that your hand slowly raises and brushes the distraction aside, as if to say "not now." Say to yourself: "In this moment, I choose to meditate." When first practicing this technique I felt as if I was at the gym doing repetitions on a weight machine, brushing aside distractions in great multiples. After some time, however, I discovered that I was able to train my mind to brush aside distractions with little effort. The moment they arrived, my mind would simply brush them away and come back into the moment.

Later, I discovered that this technique, which I used in meditation, was also very useful in daily living as a tool for staying present. At any given time, when we are distracted, we can choose to brush these distractions aside and come fully into the moment. In my life as a workshop leader and lecturer, I travel a great deal. Often, during my extensive trips, I find my mind wandering to thoughts of home. In the middle of a workshop I will begin to miss home, to think about my wife and family, and to focus on what is happening there. In that moment, I must ask myself the important questions: Is this important in influencing what I do right now or is it a distraction? Is there anything I can do about this thought right now? In both cases, the answer is no, it is a distraction, and in the middle of a trip and a workshop away from home, indulging these thoughts has only one real potential: to rob the present moment and those who are participating of my full engagement. When this occurs, I simply imagine that hand gently brushing aside the thought of home as if to say "not now." At first, this took much conscious effort but now the whole process takes but a few seconds. By training my mind, I am now able to bring myself back to the present moment within a matter of seconds. The result has been that I enjoy my workshops much more and the participants have my full attention. Curiously, my ratings as a retreat leader have gone up significantly since cultivating a greater ability to stay present.

This technique is simple but powerful. Determine if something is useful or a distraction. Decide if there is anything you want to *do* about that thought in the present moment. Gently brush it aside and come back fully into the present moment. Being in the present moment is one of those things where the old adage holds true: Practice makes perfect. The key concept is to be aware that not being in the present moment is a choice, a choice determined only by us and not by our situation.

When I was a young graduate student studying for the ministry, I completed an internship at a large nursing home on the north side of Chicago. As interns, we spent most of our time walking around from room to room visiting with elderly residents. Our supervisors had counseled us about the healing power of listening to older persons. Much later in my life, I would come to appreciate the power that focused presence has to heal people of all ages.

As interns we tried hard to cultivate deep presence and learned to look present even when thinking about a date taking place later that night. Late one afternoon I was visiting an elderly man and listening to the story of his life. After an hour or so, he said: "Do you want to know, son, what I appreciate most about you? You are the only one of the people who visits me who doesn't look at his watch."

Before your admiration for me grows, I must make a confession: That morning my watch had stopped working! At first I felt ashamed and then I tried to ask what that broken watch could teach me. I realized that, because I did not have my watch that day, I had allowed myself to be present fully and it had made that man feel loved. For years after that I did not wear a watch at all when I visited people, whether they were friends, clients, or colleagues, and I noticed that when we are not distracted, when we are fully present, when we choose to brush away all other matters, people feel cared for. What's more important, I learned that when I was fully present with others, the interactions enriched my life in deeper and more profound ways.

This ability to be fully present is critical to making the people in our lives feel loved, whether it is our children, our partners, our co-workers, our friends, or a stranger we meet on the bus. Once upon a time most of us had the natural ability to be fully present with others—and old dogs can relearn old tricks.

PART IV

Rediscovering Faith

Rediscovering innocence in the
realm of the spirit may seem a bit of an odd quest.
After all, isn't the very nature of faith to be innocent and
naïve?

For me, spirituality is not about being naïve, but about
being willing to embrace and ask the deepest and most profound
questions about life. Questions such as: What is the meaning of human
life? Does my work really matter? Is there anything beyond the day-to-
day physical realm? What is the source of deep contentment and the antidote to a loss of purpose? What does it mean to live rightly? What is the
deepest source upon which we can draw to fight a drift toward cynicism?

As children our "faith" is usually given to us: by our parents, by
our teachers, and by the society into which we happen to be born.
Second innocence in faith is to discover for ourselves what we
believe and the "answers" upon which we decide to base our life.

It is also about the courage to believe in the rightness
of the universe even after we discover the world is not
as kind as the one we thought we lived in as
children.

In this section I explore issues of faith and spirituality. As always the lessons apply to other areas of our life as well, helping us to examine important questions such as: Does what we do with our life matter? How do we keep from becoming bored at the deepest level of our soul? Are there really miracles? And how do we ultimately decide what core beliefs will guide our lives? These are the questions that all the spiritual traditions call us to ponder.

16

My First
Funeral

There is a Chinese proverb: "The one who plants the tree rarely enjoys its shade." I have shared that saying with thousands of people over the years and it seems to strike a chord. Maybe it hits home with us because we spend so much time planting trees and so little time sitting in the shade, maybe it hits home because we rarely feel we see the results of our work. Or maybe, just maybe, it is an expression of our deepest hopes, that part of us which is still innocent and idealistic, that believes one day all of our work will bear fruit and the world will be a better place because of something we did. If we are to reclaim our innocence, we must rediscover our faith in seeds, our belief in the power of something to grow even when we cannot see it. And faith above all things is about believing in the things we cannot see or hold in our hands.

I have seen this proverb play out many times. My first assignment after seminary was as assistant minister at First Presbyterian Church in Norwalk, Ohio. Within two months of my arrival, the senior minister went on a month-long European vacation. For those unfamiliar with church work, the assistant minister usually does all the work the senior minister has earned the right not to do anymore: teach Sunday school, work with the youth, facilitate endless meetings, and so forth. The senior minister does most of the "important" work: preach the Sunday sermon, conduct weddings, baptize the babies, and bury the dead.

So here I was, a young novice in my first assignment, when the funeral parlor called to say a member of our church had died. She was eighty-four-year-old Bertha Newton and I had never met her or her newly widowed husband, John. My excitement at getting to do the important work soon faded as I realized that I had attended only two funerals in my entire life, and my seminary studies had not provided even an hour of instruction on burying the dead.

Over the next several days, I pored over seminary textbooks and wrote my eulogy for a woman I had never seen alive. The day arrived and in the small-town funeral parlor, with the smell of chemicals and flowers in the air, I conducted Bertha Newton's memorial service. I was certain it was not a stellar performance. After all, even at twenty-four, I knew there were no words to heal the loss of someone who has been your partner for half a century, borne your children, and now lies before you a lifeless corpse. I remembered thinking to myself that surely the senior minister would have done a better job.

After Bertha's death, over the next twenty or so months, I visited her widower, John Newton, in his home. Our visits were not momentous. We talked about the "old days," the work he did before he retired, what his children were doing, what life was like with Bertha, the goings on at city hall, and the weather—which is always interesting in northern Ohio. It seemed to me that our visits did little to make his life richer, but I went there every six weeks like clockwork.

Almost two years after the funeral, I was assigned to a larger church as senior minister. Frantically, I made my last rounds visiting the "important" families of the church—the Chapins (big-time con-tractors), the Kniffins (lifelong members over several generations), the Jacksons (pillars of the church), and on and on. Mr. Newton was not one of these prominent people; he and Bertha had not graced the doors of the church for quite some time.

My last day, a Friday afternoon, I realized there was one more visit to be made. Driving over to John Newton's home I reflected on my two short years at this country parish and wondered if I had made any difference. All the meetings I'd attended, the homes I'd visited, the programs started, the sermons evaporated into the sounds of silence, what had I really accomplished? We sat in his small apartment, dimly lit, and had our usual conversation: the weather, the old days, Bertha. Then I announced that this would be my last visit because of my call to the larger church.

There was silence for a moment and then tears appeared in the old man's eyes. They welled up like pools, but he struggled to con-tain them. "What's wrong?" I asked.

"Oh, it's nothing," he said. "It's just that I don't believe I ever told you what a difference these visits have made for me over this past couple of years and how I've looked forward to them. And I've never told you how much it meant to me when you conducted Bertha's serv-ice. I could tell it was your first—it showed—and it was far from per-fect prose. But you poured your heart into it and I could tell you want-ed desperately to bring healing. And I know it's a great day for you, going to that big church in the city, but it's a sad day for me, a very sad day, because over the last two years I've taken great comfort from knowing that when my time came it would be you who would con-duct my service. So, before you go, let me say thank you."

As I drove away from his home that day, I wondered how many other lives I had touched, in ways I would never know. I had almost not visited him and if I had not gone to his home that day I would never have known the difference I had made. I might have left that little town thinking it had all been for naught. During all those visits I'd wondered if they were of any use—and now I knew the answer. How many other trees had I planted? How many ways had I spread seeds that one day would grow into mighty oaks?

So much of life is that way. Consider parenting. How many of us wonder if we have done a good job? If our children have caught any of the values we tried to pass on? We may never get to see the adults our children become, or know what sorts of people they might have become had we not done our good work. We may work as volunteers, trying to change deep human problems such as hunger, child abuse, poverty, environmental degradation, and we may die never knowing that the work we began with others will one day change the world.

Most of my adult life has been spent giving seminars and speeches and writing books. Most of the time I never know what difference I am making, but once in a while someone sends me a note, calls me on the phone, stops me after a talk and tells me something he or she did because of what I said. And whenever I am not sure I have made any difference I remember John Newton and think of an ancient Chinese proverb. I try to remember that I am a planter of seeds and that trees grow in their own good time.

Faith Is a Choice to Act Anyway

Faith is a way of seeing the world, a choice we make to take action even when we are unsure what difference we are making. Think of all the people who worked for civil rights when African Americans were still being lynched and persecuted; those who worked for women's rights but never lived to reap the benefits; all those who worked to stop the killing of whales and went to their resting place unaware that the practice would one day be all but banned; those who died on battlefields in World War II before it was clear that the Nazis would fall; those who fought to get children out of coal mines long before the practice ended in the developed world. And so it goes—reclaiming our idealism is to embrace in our hearts the difference we make, the faith to believe even when we do not see. Think of those who are working right now to fight injustice and build a better world, in large and small ways, those who will not live to sit in the shade.

Some time ago, I met a woman named Susan who had, years ago, worked as a colleague with a woman at a nursing home. The woman was one of those people who simply could not keep it together. She was always late to work, had a substance abuse problem and had messed up her single parenting with her twin daughters (several times the children had even been taken away by the county family services unit because of parental neglect).

My friend Susan befriended the woman and they began to socialize. After many warnings the woman was fired but Susan kept in touch.

One day the woman called Susan in a panic. Her seven-year-old twin daughters were going to a school dance and had nothing to wear, she could not afford to buy them dresses. Susan said, "Come on over and we'll go buy some material at the fabric store and we can make them dresses."

Susan made the dresses. The woman was high on something and she could hardly keep her hands from shaking. All she could do was pin the patterns here and there. But they finished just in time and took a photo of the young twins in their striking lime-green outfits.

A month or so later the woman and her daughters moved away. Years passed and, although Susan thought about the woman from time to time, she never had a sense that she had got through to her.

Sixteen years later, she ran into the woman in a mall. The woman was well dressed and looking very healthy. After a wonderful warm hug, Susan asked, "So what happened to you and your daughters?"

"Well," the woman said, "I went back to school and became a nurse and now I work over at the hospital. One of my girls just graduated from college and the other has a great job downtown. And I just became a grandmother! It is so great to see you, because you are a large part of the reason my life turned out this way."

"You see, after we fell out of touch, I never lost my girls again, never lost a job again, and got off drugs for good," the woman continued. "Do you remember that photograph we took that night of the school dance? For ten years, I kept that photograph on my refrigerator and every time it got tough, at work, at home, with temptations, I would just look at that photo and tell myself, 'If you can make those green dresses, you can get through this.' And every time I thought of quitting, that photograph helped me believe in myself again. It still sits on my refrigerator today, old, faded, but still reminding me of who I really am. Susan, if it were not for you I don't know what would have become of me. It's been such a long time, but thanks." Years ago Susan had planted a tree in the form of a simple act of kindness and that tree grew had grown out of her view to cast a mighty shadow.

So Plant Your Trees

Here is a saying to keep on your refrigerator: "Plant your trees and don't worry about sitting in the shade." Keep planting: Do good things and good works, be kind and offer sympathy, fight injustice and promote goodness, recycle your cans and newspapers, tell your kids stories with real lessons, give a few extra dollars to charity, challenge an injustice or two every week, help a friend, write a letter to the editor. Sure, it requires a bit of innocence, a willingness to believe in things you will never see. That isn't always easy, but the alternative is cynicism, resignation, and loss of hope.

By the way, I have learned over the years that people want to know the rest of the story. When John Newton died, five years later, his heirs didn't know he wanted me to conduct his service. The senior minister got the nod instead. But the senior minister was a very good man and I know he did his part. Sometimes you have to trust that you aren't the only one planting trees.

17

What Question
Rules Your Life?

My children occasionally sit down, stare at me, and speak what they perceive to be the worst of all possible human conditions: "Dad, we're bored!" Indeed, the feeling that life has lost its flavor is a significant spiritual malaise that can touch any of us at any age. So I ask myself, what is the antidote to boredom? How do we keep life feeling fresh and new? This is, at its heart, a deeply spiritual question.

My friend Steve, a mid-lifer like me, says that vacations are not what they used to be. "After all, once you've seen a few cathedrals, ruins, interesting towns, pretty beaches, and quaint shops, they all start to look the same. I feel like I've done it all before. . . ."

This could describe our experience of life. After some time, the tongue loses its ability to taste, the nose its sense of scent, the hands their sensitivity to touch, the eyes their ability to see the wonder of things. One of the ways we lose our innocence is when we begin to feel we have "done it all before." We may feel that we have experienced all that life has to give and find that our hunger has not yet been satisfied by all this tasting.

Another friend, a painter named Michael, recalls the intense scent of fresh-cut grass, the strong fragrance of newly milled lumber, and, indeed, how sharp all his senses were as a child. "What is it," he asked, "that makes life lose its freshness?" The writer of the Old Testament book of *Ecclesiastes* knew this feeling well, lamenting: "There is nothing new under the sun."

How does one escape this cycle, the experience of having done it all? Often we try to experience more things. Years of travel to tourist sites gives way to adventure travel—climbing mountains, racing cars, the ultimate spa experience, a balloon ride across mountains—the search continues. In that ever-deepening quest for a new experience, some people may actually find something that, for a time, satisfies them. But many others still find a growing sense that something is missing.

This seems to be what the Buddhists mean by the "hungry ghost." Instead of satisfying our hunger, these new experiences merely wear out the senses, so that after some time no thrill can ever be enough.

Throughout the spiritual and poetic traditions are important hints at the answer to this dilemma. Again and again, sages have pointed me toward a seemingly indisputable truth: Boredom can only be resolved by joining with something bigger than ourselves.

Asking the Right Question

Victor Frankl was a Jewish psychotherapist who spent three years as a prisoner in Auschwitz. His thoughts, captured in his book *Man's Search for Meaning*, show us why some people never lose heart—even in the most desperate of life's situations. He writes about having a faith so deep that not even a death camp could take it away. This is the ultimate test of faith.

At Auschwitz, if a prisoner wanted to commit suicide, the Nazis forbade other prisoners from attempting to stop this. Of course, people still did try to rescue those in deep despair. As a student of the human spirit, Frankl was in a unique position to observe human beings in the most dire of circumstances faced with the ultimate spiritual question: Is life worth living? Speaking of two cases of would-be suicides, Frankl writes:

> Both used the typical argument—they had nothing more to expect from life. In both cases it was a question of getting them to see that life was still expecting something from them. We found, in fact, that for one of them it was his child whom he adored and who was waiting for him in a foreign country. For the other, it was a thing, not a person. This man was a scientist who had written a series of books, a series that still needed to be finished. His work could not be done by anyone else; any more than another person could ever take the place of the father. The person who becomes conscious of the responsibility he bears towards a human being or to an unfinished work, will never throw away his life. [5]

This is a curious paradox: it is not what we expect from life, but what it expects from us that ultimately keeps us from boredom and connects us to meaning. This may help explain why there are so many miserable "searchers" going from the yoga class to the exercise regimen, then on to the painting class, the pottery lessons, the symposium on extraterrestrial wisdom. A search for what we can get from life is never as fulfilling as a search for what life expects from us!

It may also explain why most of the people I know who have lost their religious faith are people for whom God is a kind of tooth fairy. The God of our first innocence exists to give us things, to dole out favors, to keep us from being bored or hurt, to prepare our "next step" in the journey. The people I know who never lose faith are often those whose God asks much of them, one to whom they feel a deep calling to make something of their lives.

One of my best friends had been languishing for years. It seemed to me he had taken all that the world had to give him— from the silence of Zen monasteries to the pleasures of carnal experiences. He had mastered hobbies, heard the call of entrepreneurship, tried most everything there is to try, but it had not been enough. Then he learned of a program to recruit people with a great deal of life experience and train them to become teachers in the inner-city public schools. As he told me about applying for it, his eyes lit up—for the first time in years. He said, "I'm not sure you could get to those kids, but if you could, what a thing to do. . . ." In that moment, I realized what my dear friend was missing, what had driven him to the edge of the deepest existential boredom. It was not what he expected from life, but what it expected from him. He had come to a place where he no longer believed at a deep level that life had an expectation of him, a calling that must be fulfilled. And at that moment, his soul had begun to wither.

Like Trying to Train a Cat

My mother retired two years ago and has taken to sitting around watching television and training her cat. Trying to train a cat (besides being fruitless) is a sure sign of the deepest boredom. What I have observed is that my mother no longer expects anything from life and has decided that there is little in the way of joy ahead of her. But while driving one day she said to me, "What is really bugging me is that all my life there have been people who needed me. Now, no one really needs me." My mother is not unusual; we begin to die, spiritually if not physically, when we focus on what we can expect from life as opposed to what it expects from us. So I pray for my mother to rediscover what life expects of her. Anecdotal evidence is abundant that older people who stop working and who no longer feel needed age faster and die sooner than those who believe life still wants something from them.

As I went through one of the dark nights of my own soul, I sought the coaching of another ex-minister and author, John Scherer. One of his most powerful questions was this: What was my loving intention toward the world at this stage of my life? He did not ask me to ponder what I wanted from life; rather, he asked me to ponder what I wanted to *give* life and suggested that this was the secret path to the sense of purpose, the second innocence, which I sought.

We can wake up each morning and the first question that emerges is: "I wonder what life will do for me today?" But our days can begin with a very different question: "What can I give to life and the world today?" In my own practice, I have realized that we have little power over what life gives to us, but a great deal of power over what we give to it. What's more, the rewards of giving seem to be much more profound than those of receiving.

Although a case could be made for "radical" altruism, it is not my supposition that such a total focus on others is the only route to the experience of second innocence. It seems to me that there is a place for wanting new things and even for purely hedonistic pursuits. There is little of the ascetic in me, little in me that rails against the pleasures of the senses or that attempts to fight our innate desire to explore and learn. Rather, it is the insufficiency of those experiences that strikes me, the recognition of the critical place which service and being needed plays in the human psyche.

We live in a world where we are deeply in touch with the questions about what life will give us and profoundly out of touch with the question of what it expects from us. And when we know that life expects something from us, then we also know that ultimately our lives have a more lasting legacy. For that which we give is recycled, like the nutrients of a dead tree returning to the soil. What we take from life, however pleasurable it may be in the moment, is always fleeting, gone the moment the experience has ended. And this perspective, this focus on what life expects from us, can serve the young just as profoundly as it can serve older persons. My own young children always seem happiest when they are needed to help bake a cake, clean the house for company, to be of service in some way.

Many times in this book, I have tried to make the important distinction between capturing the innocence of childhood and being childish. On the current point, I believe that when we enter the world we are very focused on what life will give us. We ask it for security, for pleasure, for food, for love . . . the list goes on and on. But, as Erik Erikson described in his work on the stages of the life cycle, as we age we reach a point he calls "generativity," whereby we are focused on what we will leave behind more than what we shall take or be given.[6] This natural human journey from a focus on "self" to a focus on "other" is a critical step in the spiritual journey and we do not have to wait until we are old to take this step.

The antidote to boredom, to a loss of soul and innocence, is to ponder this question deeply: "What does life expect of me now?" Let this question touch your spirit deeply and probe you until it finds an answer. The answers will vary widely from person to person, they will change and evolve as we age and as the world's work emerges around us. Of this I am certain; the most deeply happy and fulfilled people I have met have been people who knew life expected a great deal from them. And faith, when it is mature, when it moves into its second innocence, ceases to be about what life or God will do for us, and becomes about what we can do for life. Our prayers become a prayer to be given a calling rather than an inheritance.

18

Miracles, Telephones, and Serendipity

I am asked "Do you believe in miracles?" and it occurred to me that no one had asked me that question since my days in ministry. I was taken aback. Did I believe in people being spontaneously cured of cancer, virgin births, raising of the dead, parting of seas, burning bushes, and so on? Did I believe in serendipity, synchronicity, and moments of seeming happenstance that wind up being instrumental to our path?

At one time, most of us believed in miracles just as we believed in "magic." Surely part of our childhood innocence was recognizing and appreciating the wonderful serendipity that seemed to exist in the world around us. Most of us believed in miracles when we were children, but now that I am a (sometimes) grumpy middle-aged man, long past the innocence of youth, how would I answer the question: Do I believe in miracles?

What is a miracle anyway? A working definition might go

something like this: An event out of the ordinary, an event that is unique, something that defies our logic and causes us to feel awe and wonder. A miracle is, above all, something we simply cannot explain, but that somehow gives us hope.

Before you decide whether you believe in miracles, think about this for a moment: We live on a tiny planet rotating around a massive hydrogen-fusion reactor with other planets. It's known as the solar system. That's right—the sun is not a fluorescent light in the sky, it is one absolutely enormous hydrogen reaction. It travels (yes, our entire solar system moves) through a galaxy which itself moves within a possibly infinite and ever-expanding universe. Surrounding us appears to be a lifeless void. A few microbes here and there, perhaps, but mostly rock, gas, chemical reactions, and a void with no living (let alone sentient) objects as we know them.

Look at our tiny planet from space and you see a beautiful blue sphere hung like an ornament in the vast blackness, so fragile, so alone. Astronauts have all spoken of this sudden realization when for the first time they see our world for what it really is. Come in closer and you find a planet teeming with life, from microscopic organisms to sentient beings such as ourselves who, on our best days, have deep conversations about the meaning of the universe. And how did this tiny planet come to be so fortunate? And what of the incessant manner in which life breeds more life and keeps the cycle going?

Amazement Abounds

Stepping back from the "big stuff," it seems to me that there are hints of the miraculous everywhere. We had a cat once named Nulla who became pregnant. My wife, a nurse by personality as well as formal training, knew the cat was pregnant. How she knew this, I really have no idea. A few months later we were watching television and

Nulla started to breathe heavily and came to lie next to my wife on the sofa. Somehow the cat knew that this was a fellow female, a fellow giver of life. "Stand aside, male one," Nulla seemed to be saying with her nudges. "This is women's work!" She crawled upon my wife's lap and began her journey to bear her young.

Over the next hour on my wife's lap, our curious children watch in amazement as she pushed out her kittens one by one. Each one entered the world wet and with a small meow and team of thankful onlookers. Then somehow, when the work was done, she shepherded them into a corner and lay beside them to provide warmth and sustenance. She had never seen this, never learned it in some book or been taught it by her own mother. But still she ensured the cycle was unbroken. How did this happen?

I know all about cell division and about natural selection and evolutionary principles. I am sure someone smarter than myself can create a linear trail of logic and events to explain Nulla's ability, desire, and compulsion to keep the cycle going. But deep inside I know that nothing in my logical conjectures will ever be sufficient to explain the awe I feel in the presence of such innate knowing.

And then there is this thing some people call serendipity, the intersection of things that somehow brings together events in a way that inspires hope and reminds us of unseen hands that seem to guide us.

My oldest daughter is adopted. My ex-wife and I picked her up from a hospital in Columbus, Ohio, when she was three days old. When she was three weeks old, we moved to San Diego, California, to start a new assignment.

We had both wanted children very badly and had been unable to conceive one of our own. Unfortunately, we had been struggling with our marriage for many years and when we moved to California our problems came to a head and we decided that it was time to part ways. The decision to split came when our daughter was six months old and our adoption of her just one month from being finalized.

We had both wanted children all our lives and each of us loved our daughter very much. We also knew that a divorce would not sit well with the adoption agency; it would likely mean we would lose her. For several weeks we agonized about what to do and, to my shame, we decided to lie, to tell the agency that we were still together until the adoption was final. When they called, we would say all was well. That very day we made this decision, my phone got shut off for some unexplained reason. Just shut right down, no longer in service.

I called the phone company to ask why and was told the company had "no idea, just a mistake—we'll put it back on in the morning." That night a tiny voice kept telling me that we had made the wrong decision and I told my wife that we had to tell them the truth. Whatever the cost, integrity was even more important than keeping our daughter. We would simply tell the agency that we loved her and would love to keep her even as single parents.

At 8:30 the next morning, the phone rang and my wife answered it. It was the adoption agency "just calling to check in."

My wife said, "Well, to tell the truth, things have been a little tough. John and I have been struggling for several years now and have decided that we need to split up. We know that is not good news, but we love Lena very much and would like to keep her anyway."

On the other end of the phone there was an eternity of silence. Then the woman from the agency said these words: "We heard through an anonymous caller two days ago that you two were getting a divorce. We made a decision inside the agency that we would call you and if you told us the truth we would try to help you. But if you lied we would take Lena back. I am so glad you told me the truth." Then she added: "I tried to call you all day yesterday, but your phone was disconnected." And I know, without even the hint of a shadow of a doubt, that had the phone been working that day, we would have lied.

In twenty-five years of having phone service, the phone company had never cut off my service except on the one day in all those years that it would have made a difference. Two months later we adopted Lena, and although my former wife and I have lived apart for fifteen years, she has two sets of parents who love her completely and utterly. Was this a miracle? I don't know—but I can't explain it, it did give me hope and it changed many lives.

And there have been other incidents like that; and times when I longed for a miracle and it did not come. Neither of which I can explain.

The Scientific Possibility of Miracles

Some years ago astronomers began using supercomputers to calculate the odds of there being life similar to ours elsewhere in the universe. We humans have always been fascinated with the idea of life on other worlds, of extraterrestrials. The scientists calculated the number of galaxies, the number of stars, the number of those stars likely to have planets; on and on the calculations went until they came up with the mathematical probability that life exists elsewhere. The good news is that the computer says that although very rare, there must be many other places where life has evolved as it did here on Earth. We are not so extraordinary after all.

These scientists and their colleagues started listening with giant telescopes (stuff I don't really comprehend). Using these gigantic ears, they began listening for what those other beings might be saying to us from across the universe. They were sure we would hear them, a radio signal, a television transmission, something that seemed out of the ordinary. They have been listening for more than a decade. What have they heard? Nothing. That's right—not a peep. Not even the hint of the possibility of a peep.

So they began to hypothesize (I have a Ph.D. and that is what we researchers do—we hypothesize). When we don't get the answer we expect, we look for explanations. No conclusions, not yet, but a few sobering ideas. The first hypothesis is that intelligent life does not last very long once it evolves. That is, life may have sprung up many times throughout history but, in cosmic terms, intelligent life does not hang around. Maybe civilizations blow themselves up or mess up their planet until it is unable to support the intelligent life it spawned. Who knows why, but there are plenty of possible reasons they don't hang around long enough for us to hear them. Maybe, at this given moment, we are alone. Some future civilization may listen, just as we are, but they too will hear nothing. We will have long ago snuffed ourselves out.

There is a competing theory—perhaps more sobering and awe-inspiring at the same time—that the computers may be wrong. Perhaps life is even more rare than the computer models suggest.

How might that be? Well, contemplate a few simple facts. A planet has to be within its star's small zone between too much heat and too much cold. Otherwise liquid water cannot exist, something that is essential for life as we know it. So fragile is this tiny oasis of life on Earth that if we were one degree closer to the Sun we would burn up, one degree farther away, we would freeze to death. Comets can shake and shred planets—and not just once. Bombardments from space debris can go on a very long time. For life similar to our own to exist, a world must have a similar geography and composition to the Earth's. Most planets so far detected around other stars have been massive gas giants, probably with no solid surface at all. There are many "serendipitous" occurrences that led to human beings evolving on this planet; but there is no reason for life on other worlds to develop along similar lines.

There is only one place in the universe where we know life exists, filled with sentient beings. Look around you: It's here.

So do I believe in miracles? Well, if a miracle is an extraordinary event that we cannot explain, I think we are surrounded by and living a miracle. I think the fact that I am writing this and you are pondering where you stand on the matter is a miracle. I think the fact that Nulla (and my wife) have both given birth to new life and kept the life cycle going is extraordinary. I believe that one day twenty-five years ago, grace, God or something extraordinary turned my phone off. I think the fact that this green and blue splendor floats through an otherwise deathly quiet universe is a pretty extraordinary thing. In light of the sheer wonder that we exist at all, spontaneous cures of cancer and the occasional parting of a sea are pretty unspectacular and not really worth my time to dismiss.

Maybe we are so surrounded by miracles that we start to miss them, to take them for granted. And maybe, just maybe, life would be very different, and more profoundly good, if we thought about it more often and remembered how miraculous it all is. Perhaps it is a good thing to ponder, to recognize that at this one moment in time, we may be the only ones in the entire infinite universe experiencing this miracle and the only intelligence pondering its deeper meaning.

Perhaps then we would start treating it all with just a little more respect, a little more care, a shade more awe, and maybe the miracles will keep happening.

Do I believe in miracles? Deep inside of me there is an innocent child who takes an honest look at this thing called life and simply says: Of course. And I think we ought to trust that part of us a lot more than we do, which is probably part of what second innocence is all about.

PART V

On the
Road to
Second
Innocence

One of my favorite
sayings comes from the Native American
tradition: "As you go the way of life, you will see
a great chasm. Jump! It is not as far as you think."

I have always liked the fact that it counsels: "you will
see a great chasm." Not you *might* or you *could*—but *you will*!

Throughout my life, in my faith, my work, my relationships, and daily life, I am aware that I have encountered a great
many chasms. These chasms are often the very things that challenge
our ability to stay innocent and to keep cynicism from taking over.

But I have also experienced the second part of the saying.
Whenever I have had the courage to jump, it has never been as far
as I thought it would be.

Innocence waits for us just on the other side of those
chasms. So does joy, purpose, hope, faith, wonder, and so
many of the things we seek.

These final chapters explore how we begin
the journey—and how small the chasms
sometimes truly are.

19

The Simplest Wisdom
. . . Start

Mentors are all around us. My driveway has been a mentor to me. Now, before you think me a bit eccentric, my driveway is not your average driveway. In a town of steep driveways on the side of a mountain in British Columbia, my driveway stands out as a paragon of steep driveways. Almost straight up, and a hundred feet long, those who come to our home for the first time wonder how our cars magically arrive at the top of the summit.

In summer the driveway is merely steep, but after a winter snowstorm the driveway takes on its truest character. Covered with a blanket of fresh snow, it is then that my driveway is a mentor to me.

For the first two years after we moved in, whenever it would snow, I would simply wait for the snow to melt before driving our cars back up. I could not imagine how to shovel that entire mass. Often, for weeks, we would trudge up the forty stairs through the snow, waiting for the universe to magically melt the chilly white stuff. My wife was not impressed. "I would not even know where to start," was my patented and well-practiced reply.

One year, there was a big storm while I was away. On the telephone my wife complained about the snow and the long trudge up the path. However, when I arrived home, to my utter shock, the driveway was clear. Sheepishly I asked my wife, "How did the driveway get cleared?"

"Oh," she said, "Carter and I shoveled it." Carter is our twelve-year-old son.

"But how?" I asked sheepishly.

"We just got started," she said. "The rest of it came to us from there."

For three years, every time it snowed I would look out at our driveway and wonder, "What is the perfect way to clear that driveway?" I would imagine myself sliding down to oblivion, lying in the ER with a mid-life snow-induced heart attack or driving a motorized plow up the pavement. The one thing I had never done was to start and see what happened next!

Over the years I have seen this same phenomenon in many people's lives, including my own. We wait for the perfect plan to come to us, the perfect path to wherever it is we are trying to go, when all the time the deepest wisdom we could discover would be to simply start and see what happens.

Think of all the things you plan to do someday. You know what they are, and I have my list, too. Learn a language, devote more time to charity, take it easy, exercise, be more honest, the list goes on and on. Then ask yourself this question: "What is it you are waiting for before you start?" Maybe you are waiting for the "perfect plan." The time is not quite right? I am too busy? You may try to manufacture all kinds of reasons as you bluff your way past the one true answer: There is nothing you are really waiting for, except the simple choice to get started.

We find all kinds of ways to keep ourselves from starting. I want to be more romantic and buy a library of books on how to be romantic . . . instead of simply starting somewhere, anywhere! One simple act of being romantic—that gets me going. I want to eat more healthy food and so I search the bookstores for the perfect anti-carbohydrate organic encyclopedia . . . when simply eating a little tofu today would be a fine way to start. I want to find more balance and I assure my friends incessantly that some day I will throw away this busy life . . . but the one thing I never do is simply make sure each day I do one little thing for myself.

Recently a story made the rounds in the North American media about Terry Wallis, a thirty-nine-year-old man who was in an auto accident when he was twenty years old. The crash had left him with severe brain stem injuries and paralyzed from the neck down. For over nineteen years he had been only semiconscious, reacting with an occasional grunt or nod. Through those two decades he had not spoken a single word. One day, a nurse was attending to him when she pointed to his mother and asked: "Do you know who that is?" To her shock and utter amazement he simply responded: "Mom." He then began to speak again. Several days later he was asked how he came to speak after nineteen years of silence. "I just decided to move my lips," was his simple response.

Now skeptics will say "it wasn't that simple" and they are probably right. But how many times in our lives *is* it really that simple: I just decided to move my lips! And in your own journey to innocence, what is the equivalent of simply moving your lips? What decisions and intentions are waiting for nothing except for the will to begin?

What has this do with innocence and rediscovering the joy and wonder of life? Well . . . everything. Our souls already know many of the things we must do to reclaim our ideals, to reanimate our life, but the will must turn those desires into action.

From the time we are young, we get hundreds of lessons on finishing; we attend workshops on setting goals. But when is the last time you simply had a lesson on getting started?

So here is the simplest and most profound wisdom I know: Get going! Do something, however small, to rekindle that innocent wonder that was once so native to your soul. Other steps will come to you.

One thing is for sure. Sitting inside staring at the driveway will never move that snow.

20

What If You Could Change the World?

"To achieve greatness, begin where you are,
use what you have and do what you can."
— *Arthur Ashe*

Throughout this book we have been exploring paths to a personal renaissance, avenues to rediscover the pure joy and wonder of life. But there are matters larger than the renewal of our personal lives; the entire planet longs for a reawakening of spirit and for a rekindling of idealism. A second innocence of the human species, a reclaiming of hope—these are very large things. How do we personally influence the nurturing of innocence in the broader society? How can we begin to make progress in that direction?

These questions have taken on new meaning as we have moved into the new millennium.

Toward the end of the twentieth century, there was a growing optimism in many quarters about the future of the world. The Soviet Union had collapsed and given way to a growing democratic movement, the Cold War was over and the Berlin Wall gone, the world economy was growing along with the stock market, the United Nations appeared to finally be a viable world organization, and more people were living in relative personal freedom than at any time in human history. What's more, the computer revolution had connected all of us in digital space with the promise of a more connected planet, where the Internet might contribute to a deeper understanding among people.

Of course, in our innocent optimism we ignored other, less hopeful trends. The growing disparity between rich and poor, the legion of regional conflicts that replaced the tensions between America and the USSR, the continued proliferation of nuclear weapons and other tools of mass destruction, ongoing fighting between ethnic groups in the Middle East and elsewhere, accelerating global climate change, still-rising rates of deforestation and loss of biological diversity, not to mention a world economy built on the speculation of the dot-com bubble and exaggerated examples of corporate malfeasance at companies such as Enron.

The pessimists and optimists had a great debate until the fateful day of September 11, 2001, when it became obvious that we had a good deal further to evolve before we could declare the human race to have entered a "second innocence." And events since that day have only served to reinforce that this new century brings with it many challenges.

Some months after September 11, I found myself sitting on an airplane pondering these thoughts and I became aware of how grumpy everyone around me was. The woman next to me was lamenting her boss's poor judgment in sending her on this particular sales call. The flight attendant was telling a passenger how "lousy" the airlines are now and that she was looking for another way to make a living. The man right across the aisle from me was complaining to anyone who would listen about everything imaginable—the plane, the wait, the legroom, the lack of a prompt departure, the bumpy ride. Though I consider myself a pretty positive guy, within forty-five minutes I was in the groove with my fellow passengers, bitching. The negativity reached its zenith when the flight attendant delivered the meal. The man across from me took one look at the offering and said: "Miss, this is a bad sandwich!" She stared at it a moment and then scolded it with her index finger, saying: "*Bad* sandwich! *Bad* sandwich!" She then put it back on his tray and walked away.

A few rows in front of me, in one of the bulkhead seats, was a young boy about twenty months old. All during the flight he had been trying to stand erect on his mother's lap so he could get his head above the seat and look back at all of us. Try as he might, he could not do it. Occasionally, I would see his hair, a forehead, the top of his eyebrows, but never his face. Occasionally his voice could be heard above the roar of the engines, but no full sight of him. Finally, about an hour and a half into the flight he managed to pull himself all the way up. As his chin rested on the seat and he looked back at all of us, he gave us a full-faced grin.

What followed next was astounding and profoundly simple. Within a minute of his head popping above the seat, that young boy had transformed the five rows behind him. That smile, the energy that he sent out into the cabin, the simple way he had appeared, had almost everyone in our part of the plane captivated. Several passengers were trying various tactics to get him to smile again. We all started talking about the contrast between that boy's energy and our grumpy behavior. When the "bad sandwich" guy started making comical noises to get the kid's attention, I knew that small boy had accomplished a full transformation of our section. In one single act, this child had changed the five rows around him from grumpiness to wonder.

Sitting on that airplane, I came to a powerful realization. Wherever we are in the world and whatever we do, we usually have the power to influence the people around us. Yes, we can have some influence over our town, our company, our country; but, if we are honest, most of us have a very small circle of significant influence. And although we have tremendous influence over our work colleagues, our family, the people we hang out with, our neighborhood, many of us spend most of our days talking about what somebody else is *not* doing: our boss, our mayor, our CEO, the leaders of our country.

Who Has the Power to Create Change?

This will sound a trifle Pollyanna, but I am certain it is true: The transformation of the human species, the movement toward a second innocence and renaissance for our communities, must begin— and can only begin—when each of us takes responsibility for our immediate surroundings. Only when we fully accept our power, can we hope to reclaim our idealism and counter our growing sense of impotence. It seems to me that impotence is the greatest threat to the further development of our species. And the impotence of which I speak cannot be treated with a small blue pill; it is an impotence of the spirit, a gnawing feeling that the problems we face are bigger than all of us. This impotence threatens to keep us paralyzed, doing nothing, while the hopes of humanity's future fade around us.

What is clear to me is that transformation begins wherever we find ourselves. If we want more understanding in the world we must begin building that quality in our five rows. If we want to facilitate a more innocent relationship with Mother Earth, it must start with how we impact the planet and how we talk to others about the Earth. If we desire companies to be more ethical and responsible, then we must begin by examining our own patterns of investing and purchasing and by making every effort to create ethical business practices in our place of work—beginning with our own personal behavior.

The list goes on: If we want to create a world where there are better families, we must begin with our own family, with how we treat our spouse and children. Further, we must examine how we can impact families in our sphere of influence. If we want to reduce crime, we must examine and own up to the small ways we cheat on our own ethical principles and search for ways to reach out to people within our sphere for whom crime is an option. If we want to create a more charitable world, we must begin by enhancing our own charitable behavior and become more zealous in our influence over those who interact with us on a regular basis.

So fundamental is this principle that if we fail to understand it, the human species does not stand a chance of renewal. Some people, including many intelligent observers, suggest that all through history it is only a select, small group of people who "change" the world. I do not accept this premise. If this appears to be the way the world works from time to time, it is because most of us cede responsibility to others and give up our personal power, leaving the few with inordinate influence in the void we have created. Think of an extreme example: Nazi Germany. Early in his time as Der Führer, Adolph Hitler could not have exerted his will without the complicity of hundreds of thousands of Germans, many of whom knew what they were doing was wrong. They might not have been able to change Germany, but they *could* have influenced others.

Take the crisis of ecology currently facing us, surely one of humanity's greatest challenges in this new century. Of course, government officials will make decisions that will have great influence, as will CEOs of large companies. But each of us makes personal decisions about how we use our car, how we invest, what we purchase, the kind of fuel we use, whether we recycle. These decisions in aggregate are more powerful than those of the few who have the "power" to lead. And even if the few in power were to act correctly, their success depends on our willingness to do our part. When we focus on the news in the paper instead of the news we can make in each other's lives, we abdicate responsibility and say with resignation, "If only everyone else would do it!"

Can there be a second innocence for the human family? Can we begin to reclaim the harmony with each other and with nature that is at the heart of what it means to be human? Can cynicism be thwarted and replaced with faith? Yes.

Whenever we find ourselves railing against a human dilemma, we must ask a couple of simple questions: What can I do about this thing that concerns me? Am I doing it? These are the most critical questions for all of us. If a significant majority of us began to ask such questions more regularly and sincerely, the transformational power of these simple acts would astound us.

My friend and colleague Robin Sharma loves to tell the story of one such transformational act. Oseola McCarty was a black woman who had made her living by cleaning other people's clothes. When she was in sixth grade her childless aunt got sick and she left school to care for her. She never returned. For more than seventy-five years customers brought washing and ironing to her modest frame home in Mississippi. She was paid very little, but each week she took a small part of what she earned and deposited it in the bank. She did this for decades and never took any out. When she was well into her seventies she had accumulated quite a nest egg. One day, a bank employee said: "Oseola, do you know you have accumulated quite a bit of money over the years? In fact, you now have more than $250,000." The bank's trust office then put ten dimes on the counter and asked, "If these dimes represented your money, and each one was worth $25,000, what would you like to do with those dimes?"

Oseola pondered that question and decided the following: "I will give one dime to my church, three dimes to my nieces and nephews because they need help and have been so good to me, and the rest of the dimes I would like to give to set up a college scholar-ship fund at the local college for African Americans who still dare to dream." And she did. She had little ability to change the "world," but she chose to take her savings and use them to change the people closest to her. More importantly, she focused on transforming her-self by choosing to give her entire worth to something greater than herself.

The media picked up Oseola's story and it became well known. She wound up meeting prime ministers and presidents. She received an honorary doctorate from Harvard University. Others were inspired by her story to perform their own acts of kindness, including multibillionaire Ted Turner, founder of CNN, who said that if "Oseola can give away her life savings, then I guess I could give away a billion dollars" and he did. Numerous other acts of kindness and generosity were spawned by her choice. And numer-ous African-American students are going to school because of how she acted.

A friend of mine, Rex Weyler, was a founder of Greenpeace and an editor of the *New Age Journal*. Years ago he visited a Native American chief in the plains of the Dakotas to seek advice. He told the chief that he wanted to do something about the environment, something about the growing loss of land and habitat. The chief looked him deeply in the eyes and gave him this wise counsel: "If you want to do something for the earth, find a beautiful place that you would love to live. Buy that place and protect it." So he did. He got some friends together, bought a beautiful piece of land on Cortes Island in the Strait of Georgia off Vancouver Island. He lived there and ultimately turned it into a retreat center that still exists decades later.

When I was a teenager, contemplating studying for the min-istry, I had many favorite hymns. The one I loved most had a simple verse in the chorus: "It only takes a spark to get a fire going, and soon all those around can warm up in its glowing." That boy on the plane, Oseola and her scholarship fund, my friend Rex and his land purchase, these are all examples of that hymn in action. And we must begin with transforming ourselves.

An elderly Anglican bishop was quoted as saying this toward the end of his life: "When I was young, I wanted to change the world, but the world did not want to be changed. So, in discouragement, I decided to change my community, but, to my disappointment, my community did not want to change. As I grew older, I decided that perhaps at least I could change my family, but alas I could not. Finally, as a last resort I decided to at least change myself. And then I realized, that had I begun by changing myself, my change might have influenced my family, my family might have influenced my community and my community might have begun to change the world."

I do not know what you are being called to do right now in your place of influence, but I do know this: The power of renewal is in your hands. And the ultimate act of absolute innocence, the most profound of all the ideals that if reclaimed stops cynicism right in its tracks is this: We can change the world, and fires always begin with a tiny spark.

Notes

1. e. e. cummings, "you shall above all things be glad and young."
2. Thich Nhat Hanh, *Living Buddha, Living Christ*. New York: Riverhead Books , 1995, p. 129.
3. M. Scott Peck, *The Road Less Traveled*. New York: Touchstone Books, 1998, p. 88.
4. Ming Dao-Deng, *365 Tao*. HarperSanFrancisco, 1992, p. 325.
5. Frankl, Victor. *Man's Search for Meaning*. New York: Pocket Books Edition,1963, p. 125.
6. Erik Erikson, *The Life Cycle Completed*. New York: W.W. Norton & Company, 1998, p. 176.

Discussion/Reflection Guide

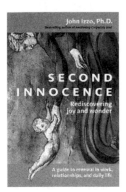

SECOND INNOCENCE
Rediscovering Joy and Wonder
John Izzo, Ph.D.

Many readers today form discussion groups to read and reflect together on a book. I think this is a great way to enhance the value of a book and to build deeper community with others. More importantly, taking time to discuss or reflect on a book makes it a great deal more likely that we will do something after reading it. It is like an insurance policy for acting on our own good intentions. The guide below works both as a personal reflection and as a group discussion guide.

Second Innocence

Discuss with others in the group ways that you have seen innocence in tension with cynicism in society? In your world (work, family, community)? And in your personal life? How have you become more cynical? What is the most difficult "ideal" for you to hold on to right now?

Dr. Izzo suggested that second innocence is a choice, one we make many times in our lives. What are some of the choices we must make now as a society to maintain innocence and thwart cynicism? What are some personal choices you need to make?

Rediscovering Wonder in the Daily Journey

This section is full of many stories about how we keep joy and wonder in daily life. What messages or stories hit home for you? What did these stories suggest might help bring joy and wonder more fully into your life?

Here are some specific questions to explore:
In what way is your life going full speed in the wrong direction? What really matters to you now? Project your life out twenty years, what might you cry about with the emotion that Mr. Jackson felt if you don't make a change now?

What did you love to do when you were young? What are some things you loved to do when you were young that need to be reclaimed?

What detours in your life or career turned out to lead to an important road? What detours are you "struggling" with right now? How could you be more open to that detour?

Mr. Thom's lesson showed us how important it is to live our ideals. How are you acting on your ideals right now? What ideals of our society are we currently in danger of ignoring? What personal ideals need claiming for you?

Trees teach us many things but most of all to let go. What must you let go of?

Rediscovering the Joy of Work

This section is full of many stories about how we keep joy in work. What messages or stories hit home for you? What did these stories suggest might help bring joy more fully into your work?

Here are some specific questions to explore:
In what ways has your job become small? What is the most noble part of your current work? What part of your job's noble purpose may be hiding from you because you see your job as "licking stamps"?

To get past our expiration date, we must see our jobs and life in new ways. In what part of your job are you trying to improve your craft? Are you in a rut in your career and work and, if so, in what way? Mrs. O'Donnell always had some part of her teaching she was working on improving; what part of your job is your focus?

Every office has one—the office troublemaker. Who is the "troublemaker" in your office? How could you "bake a cake" for them?

Dr. Izzo shared his own experience as senior minister at a church in Ohio. What are some of the ways you have lost your innocence as a leader? What part of your attitude toward others must be revised for you to lead effectively? In what area of your leadership must you be innocent and ask questions?

Rediscovering Innocence in Relationships

This section is full of stories about how we keep innocence and wonder in our relationships. What messages or stories hit home for you? What did these stories suggest might help bring more innocence into your relationships?

Here are some specific questions to explore:
What is your definition of perfect love? How have you seen innocence diminish in relationships and how have you seen the emergence of a second, deeper innocence? What methods have you used to keep innocence alive in your relationships? How might you work on the art of intimacy in your core relationships?

Presence is key to empathic relationships. How do we need to become more present?

Rediscovering Faith

This section is full of stories about how we rediscover faith. What messages or stories hit home for you? What did these stories suggest might help rekindle your faith?

Here are some specific questions to explore:
What part of your innocent faith has changed or died? How has your faith matured and incorporated harder truths about life? What trees have you planted and only seen the results years later? What miracles and serendipity have you experienced that have rekindled your innocence? What does life expect of you at this time?

On the Road to Second Innocence

What do you need to do to get started in rekindling innocence, joy, and wonder? What is it that keeps you "watching the driveway"?

Each of us has the ability to influence the rows around us much like the young boy did on that airplane. How could you get a fire going right now? What part of yourself must be transformed for you to contribute more deeply to others?

Index

About the
Author

Since age 12 John Izzo wanted to "change the world." Now as a modern thinker, change agent, and best-selling author he can proudly look back on 20 years of facilitating deeper conversations about values and work, life, faith, leadership, and success. He spent six years as a parish minister before pursuing the corporate world and advising thousands of leaders, professionals, and front-line colleagues to foster workplaces of excellence, purpose, learning, and renewal. Each year he speaks at more than 100 corporate and association events on improving the quality of work and life. His unique ability to understand what makes for a great workplace has made him one of North America's most sought after advisors on creating engaging workplaces where leaders and professionals at all levels find deeper meaning and purpose. His clients have ranged from high tech to high touch, hotels to hospitals, and from government agencies to entrepreneurial start-ups. In each case, his beliefs, wisdom, and experience have helped people discover deep and practical ways to create engaged vital teams and intentional positive lives.

Dr. Izzo is the author of three other books: *Awakening Corporate Soul: Four Paths to Unleash the Power of People at Work* (Fairwinds Press, 1997), *Awakening Corporate Soul: The Workbook for Teams* (Fairwinds Press, 1999), and *Values Shift: The New Work Ethic and What It Means for Business* (Fairwinds Press, 2001). He has traveled the world advising, speaking, and doing research on workforce trends, positive corporate cultures, and connecting with like-minded thinkers also creating powerful change.

He obtained dual Master's degrees in Theology and Divinity from the University of Chicago, his Ph.D. from Kent State University, and has served on the faculties of two major universities. His opinions, research, and expertise have been widely published and featured in media including Fast Company, CNN, Wisdom Network, Canada- AM, ABC World News, *The Wall Street Journal*, *The New York Times*, *The Globe and Mail*, and the *National Post*. His clients include Kaiser Permanente, Mayo Clinic, Fairmont Hotels, Astra Zeneca, Coca-Cola, Hewlett-Packard, IBM, Toys R Us, Verizon, Duke Energy, and the Department of National Defense.

Born and raised on the east coast of the United States, Dr. Izzo now lives with his wife and children in the mountains outside Vancouver, Canada.

Working with
Izzo Consulting, Inc.

Izzo Consulting, Inc. is dedicated to improving the quality of work and life through leading edge training, consulting, and resource materials as well as tools and resources that support personal growth and well-being.

If you wish to work with John Izzo he does work in the following ways:

- **Keynote Speaking** appearances to associations, corporations, foundations, or other groups who want to create change.
- **Coaching** one-on-one for personal, professional and/or spiritual development. These Intensives are intended for individuals committed to taking their lives, careers, or workplaces to the next level.
- **Coaching Workshops for Teams** of leaders and colleagues who want to work together more supportively and cohesively.
- **Executive Team Advising Relationships** on developing a

sustainable, values-driven culture and the initiatives needed to create organizational change.

- **Spiritual Retreats** that explore and discuss topics of mid-life, leadership, and issues of the heart and mind.
- **Wilderness Spiritual Retreats** that take leaders into the Canadian wilderness to explore issues of personal development while having a unique experience in unparalleled natural beauty.

To book John Izzo as a Keynote Speaker for your next event— call our toll free number: 1-877-913-0645

Contact information:
Izzo Consulting, Inc.
P.O. Box 668
Lions Bay, BC V0N2E0
Canada
Office: 604-913-0649
Fax: 604-913-0648
e-mail: info@izzoconsulting.com
www.izzoconsulting.com

Visit the official book web site where you can read other stories, post your own stories, and connect with people who are also on the journey to a *Second Innocence.*

www.secondinnocencebook.com

We would love to hear from you!

Time and the Soul
Where Has All the Meaningful Time Gone—and Can We Get It Back?

Jacob Needleman

Through intriguing stories—of a psychiatrist going back in time to encounter his younger self; of a mysterious meeting in the Asian desert; of the mystic master Hermes Trimegistus; as well as stories from the Bhagavad-Gita, the Bible, and other wisdom traditions—Needleman illuminates the great mystery of time and helps us resolve our increasingly dysfunctional relationship to it.

Paperback • ISBN 1-57675-251-8 • Item #52518 $12.95

Turning to One Another
Simple Conversations to Restore Hope to the Future

Margaret J. Wheatley

Bestselling author Margaret Wheatley explores the power of conversation to create real change. She defines the necessary conditions for supporting meaningful dialogue that make change possible, offers points for reflection, and presents questions that help people begin such meaningful dialogues and lead them to share their deepest hopes and fears.

Paperback original • ISBN 1-57675-145-7 • Item #51457 $16.95

Leadership and Self-Deception
Getting Out of the Box

The Arbinger Institute

Leaders can be the source of leadership problems or the source of leadership success. The authors examine this surprising truth, identify self-deception as the underlying cause of leadership failure, and show how any leader can overcome this to become a catalyst of success.

Hardcover • 1-57675-094-9 • Item #50949 $22.00
Paperback • 1-57675-174-0 • Item #51740 $14.95

Berrett-Koehler Publishers
PO Box 565, Williston, VT 05495-9900
Call toll-free! **800-929-2929** 7 am-9 pm EST

Or fax your order to 802-864-7627
For fastest service order online: **www.bkconnection.com**

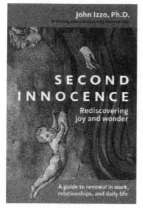